KEN NEWTON

Improvise, Adapt, Succeed®

Leadership and business lessons for turning uncertainty into clarity and results

To my wife, for always encouraging me

To Mum and Dad, for always supporting me

To Helen, for helping achieve my dreams

Contents

Foreword

Leadership is often spoken about in terms of authority, strategy, or outcomes. Far less often is it described in terms of continuity — what is passed on, what is strengthened in others, and what endures beyond the individual.

I have known Ken not only as a friend, but through a relationship that has spanned mentorship in both directions. He has invested time and guidance into my son's development, and I have had the privilege of supporting him in different seasons of his own journey. That reciprocal dynamic speaks to something important: leadership is never static. It evolves. It matures. It deepens.

Improvise, Adapt, Succeed® reflects that evolution.

This is not a book built on theory alone. It is shaped by lived experience — from remote Western Australia to military service, business, and advisory roles in complex environments. Ken does not position himself as someone who always had the answers. Instead, he shares the patterns that emerged when conditions were uncertain, when plans shifted, and when pressure demanded composure rather than reaction.

What stands out most is the clarity of thought running through these pages. Improvisation is not recklessness; it is movement when perfect conditions do not exist. Adaptation is not surrender; it is refinement in response to reality. And success, as Ken thoughtfully explains, matures into stewardship

— a responsibility for what continues after you.

This book invites leaders to think beyond short-term wins. It challenges them to build capability, strengthen systems, and respond deliberately when the environment changes — because it always does.

I have seen the principles in this book lived out, not just written down. They are grounded, tested, and practical.

For leaders navigating uncertainty, this work offers not noise, but clarity.

— David Rogers Certified Management Consultant

Preface

This book is not a step-by-step manual.

It is a lens.

It is written for leaders, founders, and decision makers who want to think more clearly, act more deliberately, and build organisations that endure beyond individual effort. It is for those operating in complex environments where certainty is fleeting, pressure is constant, and progress rarely follows a linear path.

Improvise – Adapt – Succeed® does not offer shortcuts. It offers a perspective shaped by lived experience — across military service, business, and advisory roles in environments where plans shifted and pressure exposed both strength and fragility.

Over time, a pattern emerged.

When clarity strengthens, decisions improve.

When adaptability matures, systems stabilise.

When leadership steadies under pressure, organisations endure.

This book is structured in four parts.

Part One explores improvisation — not as an impulsive reaction, but as disciplined movement when conditions refuse to cooperate.

Part Two examines adaptation — the deliberate refinement of thinking, systems, and leadership as reality evolves.

Part Three considers success — not as a result to claim, but as stewardship to sustain.

Part Four brings these ideas into application, offering practical tools and structured reflection to help translate perspective into action within your own leadership and organisational context.

Reflection is intentional throughout. Each section invites you to pause, assess your environment honestly, and consider how these principles apply in practice.

Leadership is not revealed by control alone, but by how people and systems perform when pressure is applied.

If you are prepared to think clearly, adjust deliberately, and lead steadily in uncertain conditions, this lens is offered to you.

— Ken Newton

Introduction

Most of us don't struggle because we lack ideas.

We struggle because the world changes faster than our plans.

You make a decision. You commit. You start moving forward — and then something shifts. A market tightens. A system breaks. A person leaves. A health issue appears. The neat line you expected your life or business to follow suddenly bends.

When that happens, we tend to ask the same questions:

Did I make the wrong decision?

Should I stop and rethink everything?

Why does this feel harder than it should?

This book was written for those moments.

Not to give you a checklist or a five-step formula, but to offer a way of thinking — one grounded in lived experience, constraint, and adaptation rather than theory alone.

The stories you're about to read come from my life: childhood, remote Western Australia, military service, business, leadership, and advisory work. They aren't presented as examples to copy, but as prompts to reflect on your own journey. What worked. What didn't. What you had to improvise when the plan fell apart.

Over time, I came to realise that the pattern shaping my life

and work could be described in three simple words:
Improvise. Adapt. Succeed.

Improvise	Adapt	Succeed
Gets you moving when structure is missing.	Makes it repeatable when the environment changes.	Creates legacy when success has matured.
Signs you're there:	Signs you're there:	Signs you're there:
Heroic work	Routines merge	Runs without you
Workarounds	Gaps still show	Culture holds
You solve it	You still approve	Systems created
Risk if stuck:	**Risk if stuck:**	**Risks if stuck:**
Burnout	Fragility	Stagnation

Improvisation gets you moving when conditions aren't ideal.

Adaptation helps you stabilise what works as the environment changes.

Success, when it matures, becomes less about personal achievement and more about what survives you.

This book isn't about chasing success at all costs. It's about navigating uncertainty with intent, building capability instead of dependency, and learning how to respond when things don't go to plan — because they rarely do.

You don't need to read this book from cover to cover in one sitting. Some chapters may resonate more than others, depending on where you are right now. There are moments of story, moments of reflection, and moments where you may recognise yourself more clearly than you expected.

If there's one thing I hope you take away, it's this:

You don't need perfect conditions to make progress.

You need clarity about the outcome, respect for your constraints, and the willingness to move — allowing the rest to be figured out along the way.

I

Part One

Improvise

According to the Cambridge Dictionary, improvise means:
To invent or provide something at the time when it is needed without having already planned it."
— Cambridge Dictionary

In the chapters that follow, I'll show how deliberate improvisation strengthens leadership when conditions refuse to cooperate.

1

A moment of necessity

Improvisation

Remember when we were kids, and nothing really worried us?

We didn't need much. We didn't overthink. We didn't require the "right" tools, perfect conditions, or a five-step plan. We made do with what we had, and somehow, it was enough.

I can still hear my mother telling my wife years later, "Give him a clothes peg and a leaf, and he'll be entertained for hours!" I wasn't fussy. I didn't need the latest toy or the biggest set. I could turn almost anything into something.

Improvisation comes naturally to children. It's instinctive. It's creative. It's efficient.

Somewhere along the way, that changes.

As we grow older, we tend to lose the willingness to improvise the way we once did. In business, improvisation often gets dressed up in more acceptable language: adapting to market conditions, aligning with trends, responding to competitors, or managing change.

Call it what you like. It's still the same core skill: making good decisions with imperfect information, in real time, using what you already have.

The stories in this book come from my childhood and adult life. They're not polished corporate case studies. They're real moments, shaped by real constraints. My hope is that, as you read them, you'll see how reflecting on your own experiences can help recognise how you already adapt when things don't go to plan, and re-learn improvisation and apply it in today's business environment, where certainty is rare and the goalposts often move.

The instinct to improvise and find another way showed up early in my life.

When I was four years old, I underwent a medical test.

I was born with a few health challenges, but to me, life felt normal. Looking back, I can see a pattern that followed me for years: when something didn't work the expected way, I found another way.

During a routine doctor's visit, it was suspected that I might be hearing impaired. Further testing was required. So there I was, four years old, sitting in a specialist's office with my mother, surrounded by people in white coats.

One of the tests was simple, at least on paper. Someone would stand behind me and click their fingers, clap their hands, or use a small clicker. The expectation was that the child would turn their head toward the sound.

After several attempts, the medical team concluded I was deaf.

My mother wasn't prepared to accept that. She challenged the result and demanded a second opinion. After some firm language and refusal to be brushed off, a second medical team agreed to come in.

This was the 1970s. Medical authority was treated like gospel. Parents, especially mothers, were expected to comply. "The doctors know best." End of discussion.

But my mother wasn't having it.

The new team repeated the test. Again, someone stood behind me. Click. Clap. Noise.

And again, I didn't turn my head.

My mother insisted that one doctor stand where she was standing and watch what was actually happening during the test.

Reluctantly, they did.

The test started again.

Behind me: click, clap, noise.

This time, the observing doctor saw what my mother had seen all along. I wasn't turning my head, but I was moving my eyes in the direction of the sound. I was tracking it. I was responding — just not in the way the process demanded.

The doctor said simply, "The child is not deaf."

And that was that.

What the test measured wasn't hearing.

It measured compliance with a preferred method.

That moment has stayed with me because it highlights something we still struggle with in business today.

We confuse the process with the outcome.

We confuse "the way we've always done it" with the way it must be done.

We confuse non-conformity with incompetence.

And sometimes, we label people or businesses as failing when, in reality, they're solving the problem differently.

Here's the lesson: achieving a result can be done in more

than one way.

I was four years old. I didn't have a philosophy or a framework. I simply didn't perform to the expected script, and yet the outcome was still there.

In adult life, I've seen the same dynamic play out in workplaces and boardrooms. A new approach gets shut down because it doesn't match the accepted method. A business owner gets criticised for not doing things the "proper" way, even while growing, remaining profitable, and delivering value.

Improvisation is the courage to separate outcomes from methods.

That matters now more than ever.

Small to Medium Enterprises operate in environments that are rarely stable. Cost pressure, supply disruptions, staff shortages, technology changes, compliance shifts — and the occasional surprise that knocks the week sideways. You can have a plan, and you should, but you also need the ability to move when reality changes.

Improvisation isn't chaos. It isn't winging it.

It's resourcefulness with intent.

It's the ability to ask:

- What outcome are we actually trying to achieve?
- What constraints are real, and which ones are assumed?
- What do we already have that can be repurposed?
- What's the smallest move we can make that creates momentum?

Improvisation is also deeply linked to how we view people.

As a business grows, you'll encounter different working styles and decision speeds. Some people follow the process perfectly.

Others get the result by taking a different route.

One isn't automatically better than the other.

The risk is building a culture that rewards obedience over outcomes. When people fear being punished for trying something different, they stop taking initiative. Over time, the business becomes fragile — not because people lack capability, but because the safest move becomes doing nothing outside the script.

That's why diversity of thought matters. Not just demographics, but differences in how people interpret situations and move toward outcomes. In small and medium businesses, those differences are fuel for resilience.

Improvisation is also a leadership skill.

A leader who improvises well doesn't demand "turn your head." They look for evidence of hearing. They focus on outcomes, not theatre. They provide enough structure to stay aligned, and enough flexibility to stay effective.

They create clarity around the destination while allowing multiple routes to get there.

For an SME owner, this shows up quickly:

- Redesigning a workflow because the old one no longer fits your volume.
- Changing how you quote or invoice because cash flow has tightened.
- Training a team member differently because they learn by doing.
- Reworking a service offering because clients now value speed and certainty.
- Using existing relationships to solve a capability gap instead of hiring immediately.

Improvisation is often what keeps you moving while others wait for perfect information.

And that's the final point I want to land in this opening chapter.

Improvisation isn't about being "outside the box."

It's about realising the box was never the point.

The point was the result.

At four years old, I "failed" a test because I didn't do what was expected — yet I still gave the correct response, more efficiently. Why turn my whole head when my eyes could do the job?

Sometimes improvement looks like less motion, more outcome.

So if you take nothing else from this chapter, take this:

When a process tells you something is impossible, check whether it's measuring what actually matters.

Because in business — your business — unconventional doesn't automatically mean wrong.

It might mean better.

All you need to do is think differently... and move your eyes.

2

Learning to move differently

Improvisation Under Constraint

A few years later, at the age of six, improvisation took on a very different meaning for me.

It was no longer about creativity or curiosity.

It was about necessity.

I had a terrible sense of balance. I walked differently from the other children and had speech issues that set me apart. After many visits to doctors and specialists, I was diagnosed with a motor form of Cerebral Palsy. The effects were physical and visible. My gait was unusual, I walked on tiptoes, unable to put my heels down, which threw my balance off and made simple movements harder than they should have been.

At that age, I did not have the language to explain any of this.

I only knew I moved differently.

What I also knew was that I still wanted to be a kid.

The diagnosis did not stop me from running up and down the street with the other children, although I never won any races. It did not stop me from riding my bike, even if I fell more often. It did not stop me from playing Frisbee in the backyard or the park, even if my coordination was not great. I participated, adapted, and kept going.

Looking back now, that matters. Because the instinct was not to withdraw or wait until conditions were perfect. It was to participate anyway.

That instinct — to keep moving when conditions aren't ideal — is one most business owners recognise immediately.

At the age of seven, the doctors decided surgery was required to stretch my Achilles tendons in both legs. The procedure was successful, but the recovery was confronting. I woke up with twenty-five stitches, fourteen in my left leg and eleven in my right, and plaster casts on both legs that extended above the knee.

The instructions were clear. I was to be in plaster for six weeks, on strict bed rest.

Please cast your mind back to when you were seven years old. How well did you cope with being stuck in bed when you did not want to be there?

I wanted to be outside. I wanted to be with the other kids. I wanted to ride bikes, chase Frisbee, and do all the things that felt normal to me. Instead, I was stuck in bed with my legs elevated on cushions to reduce swelling, staring at the ceiling and counting the cracks.

I was bored. I was frustrated. And more than anything, I felt trapped.

This is where improvisation under constraint really begins.

After about a week, the plaster was reshaped and shortened to below my knees. That small change altered everything. It was still restrictive, but it created just enough space to think differently.

I began twisting and fidgeting in bed until my legs were close to the edge. I pushed the cushions away. I wriggled around until my legs were hanging over the side of the bed. Carefully, slowly, I lowered myself onto the cushions on the floor.

From there, I rotated my body so my legs slid under the bed frame. If you recall the old metal-framed single beds with springs that resembled cyclone fencing, you will understand why this was neither elegant nor comfortable. Using my arms and my heels — which were now set flat in the plaster as if I were standing — I scooted backwards.

Out of the bedroom.

Down the hallway.

Towards the kitchen.

Thank goodness it was the 1970s, and linoleum was everywhere.

I was not supposed to be there. The doctor was not happy when he later saw that I had worn a hole through the heel of the plaster. Mum was shocked to see me out of bed.

But I was smiling.

I was mobile.

I was free.

I had improvised a new form of transport.

The next adjustment came quickly. Because I could not use crutches and still couldn't square my gait, wooden blocks were added to the soles of the plaster casts. This allowed me to stand flat-footed with assistance and begin walking properly, even while still in plaster.

What none of us expected was that the wooden blocks fitted neatly over the pedals of my bike.

Look out, world, here I come.

Now, let us pause the story for a moment. The way I improvised as a child—adapting to my circumstances and finding movement despite constraints—mirrors the challenge business owners face every day.

Improvisation is often romanticised as creativity or innovation, but my experience shows it is typically born out of necessity—just as it is for small and medium-sized businesses facing real-world limits.

You do not improvise when everything is going well.

You improvise when cash is tight.

When staff are unavailable.

When supply chains break.

When a key client leaves.

When the rules change.

Constraint forces choice.

In my case, the constraints were physical. I could not walk normally. I could not leave the bed. I could not use crutches. I could not wait six weeks without losing my mind.

So the question became simple and practical: given what I have, what can I do?

This is the same question SME owners face every day, whether they articulate it this way or not.

You rarely have unlimited resources. You do not have spare teams waiting on the bench. You do not have perfect systems or endless capital. What you do have is experience, relationships, ingenuity, and the ability to decide.

Improvisation under constraint is not reckless.

It is adaptive.

Notice something important in this story. I did not deny the constraint. I did not pretend that the plaster was not there. I worked with it. I used it. I found ways to move within it.

This is where many businesses get stuck.

They spend enormous energy fighting constraints instead of designing around them. They complain about limitations rather than asking how those limitations can inform smarter decisions. They wait for the constraint to disappear before acting.

In business, constraint-aware improvisation may appear as redesigning your service offering because you cannot hire fast enough. It might mean bundling services differently because your clients are price-sensitive. It might mean automating part of your workflow because you cannot afford another salary yet, it might mean partnering instead of expanding, or simplifying instead of scaling.

The businesses that survive are not always the largest or have better resources.

They are often the most responsive.

There is another layer to this story that matters for leaders. Improvisation is not always neat. It does not always follow the rules. It may even upset the authorities.

The doctor was unhappy. The hole in the plaster was evidence that I had not complied; from his perspective, I had failed the recovery plan.

From my perspective, I had solved a problem.

In business, leaders need to be careful not to punish outcomes because the method was unexpected. When you measure compliance instead of results, you discourage initiative. When you value rules over reality, you teach people to stop thinking.

Improvisation under constraint requires trust.

As a leader, this means being clear with what matters and flexible in how it is achieved. It means understanding the difference between safety-critical rules and habitual processes.

It means recognising that some of the best solutions will not look like what you would have designed yourself.

The wooden blocks were not part of the original plan.

Neither was the bike.

Yet both accelerated recovery and capability.

This brings us to another practical lesson for SMEs. Improvisation is often incremental. It builds step by step.

First, I got out of bed.

Then I moved around the house.

Then I stood.

Then I walked.

Then I rode.

Each step created information. Each adjustment revealed the next possibility.

In business, this is how momentum is built. Not through grand reinvention, but through small, deliberate moves that expand what is possible. You test. You observe. You adjust.

Improvisation under constraint also builds confidence.

Every time you solve a problem with what you have, you reinforce the belief that you can handle the next one. That belief is contagious. Teams feel it. Clients sense it. Decisions get made faster.

Over time, this becomes culture.

A culture that says, "We will figure it out."

A culture that sees constraint not as failure, but as information.

When I look back on that period of my life, I do not remember the frustration as much as I remember the determination. I remember wanting to move, wanting to participate, wanting to keep up.

That desire did not disappear as I got older. It simply changed context.

In business, the stakes are higher. There are livelihoods involved. There is responsibility. But the principle remains the same.

Improvisation is not about breaking rules for the sake of it.

It is about finding movement when stillness is imposed.

For small and medium-sized businesses, this skill is not optional.

It is foundational.

You will not always have the luxury of time.

You will not always have clarity.

You will not always have agreement.

What you will have is constraint.

And within that constraint, you will have a choice.

Sometimes all it takes is reshaping the plaster.

Sometimes it takes wearing a hole in the heel.

Improvisation under constraint gets you moving.

What matters next is what you do once movement becomes possible.

3

Making something from nothing

Improvisation When the Environment Changes

My sister is seven years older than I. Because of the age gap, we didn't do many things together — at least not things that I enjoyed.

I don't consider being tied to a chair and used as a mannequin so my sister could practise her St John Ambulance First Aid training enjoyable.

My sister did.

In many ways, I grew up like an only child.

That sense of being self-directed became more pronounced because of where we lived. We left Balga, in Perth, heading to the Pilbara — specifically, Nickel Bay in Karratha. But before suburban streets and brick houses, before Nickel Bay, my mum, dad, sister and I lived on Nanutarra Station.

Nanutarra Station sits about 280 kilometres south of Karratha, roughly 80 kilometres from the Onslow turn-off, and about seven hours north of Carnarvon in Western Australia.

It is remote in a way that is difficult to fully appreciate unless you have lived it.

There were no neighbouring houses.

No shops around the corner.

No playgrounds.

No school gate with parents dropping kids off each morning.

And there was certainly no internet.

What we had instead was distance, isolation, and a very different rhythm of life.

For my parents, it was a major adjustment. For my mum especially, it meant stepping into roles she had never trained for and never expected to hold.

One of those roles was teacher.

Until then, school had meant a building, classmates, desks, bells, and teachers who specialised in teaching. On the station, none of that existed.

What we were introduced to instead was something we had never heard of before.

School of the Air.

For those unfamiliar with it, School of the Air is a form of distance education designed for children living in remote areas. Schoolwork is completed at home. Lessons are guided by correspondence. And once a week — assuming atmospheric conditions were favourable — students attended class via two-way radio.

Yes. Radio.

At a set time, children across vast distances would tune in, call in, respond to questions, and participate in lessons through a crackly connection that depended entirely on weather, signal strength, and a bit of luck.

This was a huge change for me.

It was also a huge change for my mum.

She was not a trained teacher. She had not signed up to run a classroom. Yet suddenly, she was responsible for lesson plans, structure, discipline, encouragement, and learning outcomes.

There was no curriculum portal to log into.

No learning management system.

No YouTube tutorials.

No online forums.

There was printed material, a radio, and determination.

Improvisation was not optional.

It was required.

From my perspective as a child, this was confusing and, at times, frustrating. Learning happened at the kitchen table. Mum was both parent and teacher. Classmates existed only as voices on a radio.

From my mum's perspective, it was a crash course in adaptability.

She had to interpret instructions written for trained educators and translate them into something workable in a home environment. She had to manage behaviour, motivation, and learning without the structures she was used to relying on.

And she had to do it in isolation.

Looking back now, this period is one of the clearest examples of improvisation driven by environmental change.

No one asked whether this was ideal.

And that distinction matters in business.

In SMEs, change often arrives without permission. You do not get to vote on whether the environment shifts. Market conditions change. Regulations change. Geography changes. Customer behaviour changes.

Sometimes the entire operating context changes, and you

are left to figure it out in real time.

That is exactly what happened on Nanutarra Station.

The environment changed, so the system had to change.

The tools were limited. The support was distant. The expectations remained.

And somehow, it worked.

Not perfectly. Not smoothly. But well enough.

This is an important point. Improvisation does not require perfection.

It requires sufficiency.

It requires asking, *"What will work here, given where we are?"*

This question sits at the heart of business stabilisation.

Many SME owners I work with feel pressure to implement "best practice". They read articles, attend workshops, and compare themselves to businesses operating in very different environments.

Yet, best practice in the wrong context can become bad practice quickly.

What works in a metro-based business with scale, capital, and specialist teams may not work in a regional SME, a family business, or a business under cash-flow pressure.

Context matters.

And improvisation is how you honour context without giving up on the outcomes.

School of the Air taught me something else as well, although I didn't have the words for it at the time.

It taught me that learning, progress, and performance do not always look the way we expect.

Some weeks, the radio connection was clear. Other times, it was patchy or unusable. Lessons were adapted. Expectations shifted. Progress was uneven.

But learning still happened.

That lesson will become important later, when we talk about **Adapt**. For now, it's enough to recognise that improvisation often begins with accepting that the environment has changed — and resisting the urge to force old methods into new conditions.

Eventually, we moved again.

This time to Nickel Bay, in Karratha.

Compared to station life, Nickel Bay felt busy; There were houses. Streets. Brick walls. Neighbours.

And for me, something else appeared again.

Time.

Lots of it.

Growing up in Nickel Bay, with my sister still significantly older than me, I again found myself creating my own entertainment.

And that is where the peg-sledge incident took place.

Cast your mind back for a moment. Who remembers the movie *Tron*?

Those light bikes race along glowing lines at breakneck speeds, leaving trails behind them. To a kid, it was mesmerising. Fast. Clean. Precise.

What I didn't realise at the time was that a standard brick-and-mortar house could be repurposed into something similar.

One day, Mum asked a very practical question.

"Where have all the clothes pegs gone?"

Not the plastic ones you see today. These were the old wooden pegs, with a spring in the middle holding the two halves together.

In true child fashion, I responded with complete sincerity. "I don't know."

The truth revealed itself shortly afterwards.

Outside, Mum found me sitting near the wall. I had removed the springs from the pegs and discarded them over my shoulder. Using the two wooden halves, I was dragging them along the mortar lines between the bricks, re-enacting *Tron* scenes in my head.

The bricks were the grid.

The mortar lines were the tracks.

The pegs were my bikes.

Mum did not see innovation.

Mum saw missing pegs.

I was banned from taking any more.

At the time, it was just a child's imagination at work. Looking back now, it perfectly illustrates how improvisation often shows up.

I didn't see clothes pegs.

I saw potential.

And that difference in perspective is exactly what separates businesses that stabilise and grow from those that stall.

Improvisation is not about ignoring constraints.

It is about working within them creatively.

On the station, the constraint was distance and isolation.

In Nickel Bay, the constraint was limited resources and boredom.

In both cases, the response was the same.

Re-imagine what you have.

In business, this shows up constantly.

You may not have the budget for a new hire, but you may have an underutilised capability in your existing team.

You may not have the capital for new systems, but you may have inefficient processes that can be simplified.

You may not be able to expand yet, but you may be able to stabilise and strengthen your core offer.

Improvisation is often the act of repurposing rather than replacing.

This is particularly important for SMEs during periods of uncertainty.

When things feel unstable, the instinct is often to add more — more systems, more activity, more ideas.

But stabilisation often comes from doing fewer things better.

Improvisation asks different questions:

- What do we already have that works?
- What is underutilised?
- What assumptions are we carrying that no longer fit our environment?
- What can we simplify without losing value?

This is where rigidity becomes a hidden risk.

When leaders cling to "the way it should be" instead of responding to the way it is, they create friction. Teams feel it. Customers feel it. Decision-making slows.

Improvisation, by contrast, restores movement.

It allows progress without waiting for ideal conditions.

That does not mean abandoning planning. It means holding plans lightly.

As Helmuth von Moltke famously observed, *"No plan of operations reaches with any certainty beyond the first encounter with the enemy's main force."*

Business is no different.

Plans give direction. Improvisation keeps you moving when reality intervenes.

Looking back, there is a clear thread through these early experiences.

At Nanutarra Station, learning happened without a classroom.

In Nickel Bay, entertainment happened without toys.

Movement happened without perfect tools.

In each case, the outcome mattered more than the method.

For small and medium businesses, this is a critical mindset.

Stabilisation and growth do not come from blindly copying another model. They come from understanding your environment, using what you have, and being willing to adapt your approach.

Sometimes the solution is not a new strategy.

Sometimes it is seeing your existing assets differently.

Sometimes it is turning pegs into sledges.

And sometimes, it is recognising that the environment has changed — and accepting that improvisation is not a failure of planning.

It is a response to reality.

That idea will become even more important as we move into the next section of this book.

Improvisation gets you moving. **Adaptation is what keeps you moving forward.**

And that distinction is everything.

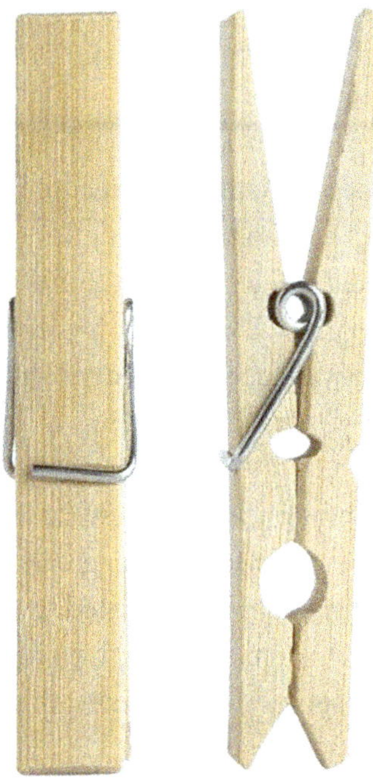

4

Reflection

Patterns of Improvisation

Before moving on, it's worth pausing.

Not to revisit the stories in detail, but to notice what they have in common.

Across the experiences in this first section, improvisation did not show up as brilliance or innovation. It showed up as response. It emerged when conditions did not match expectations, and waiting was not an option.

Improvisation appeared under constraint.

When the environment dictated terms.

When systems were missing.

When comfort and certainty were unavailable.

And yet, movement happened anyway.

This matters because improvisation is often misunderstood as a personality trait — a talent or creative gift that some people have and others don't. The reality is far more practical.

Improvisation is often simply the act of responding honestly to what is in front of you.

A child responds differently to a test.

A family adjusts to life without modern conveniences.

A young mind re-imagines everyday objects to create momentum.

None of these moments involved a grand plan. They involved awareness, agency, and a willingness to act within constraints.

That same pattern plays out in business every day.

Most small and medium business owners don't wake up trying to be innovative. They wake up trying to make things work. They solve problems with incomplete information. They repurpose what they already have. They adjust on the run.

That *is* improvisation.

And if you're reading this, there's a good chance you're already doing it, even if you don't call it that. You might simply call it "running the business."

Look closely, and familiar themes will appear:

- You've made decisions without complete data.
- You've created workarounds when systems fell short.
- You've relied on judgement more than process.
- You've stepped in personally to keep things moving.

These are not signs of poor leadership.

They are signs of responsiveness.

Improvisation often keeps a business alive in its early stages. It helps organisations survive disruption and uncertainty when structure is thin or absent.

But improvisation has a limit.

Over time, constant responsiveness becomes exhausting. The same behaviour that once created momentum can begin to create fragility. Knowledge stays trapped in individuals. Decisions remain reactive. Progress depends on effort rather than design.

This is where many capable business owners begin to feel stretched.

Nothing is failing, but nothing is settling either.

Growth feels possible, and risky.

That tension is the signal.

It doesn't mean improvisation was wrong.

It means the environment has changed.

Before moving into the next section, consider these questions quietly:

Where in your business are you still improvising because you haven't yet adapted?

* * *

Which problems keep reappearing because the underlying structure hasn't changed?

Where does progress rely too heavily on you being present, attentive, and available?

These questions are not criticism. They are orientation.

They help you see where improvisation has taken you as far as it can — and where a different response is now required.

Adaptation does not replace improvisation.

It builds on it.

Improvisation gets you moving.

Adaptation determines whether you can keep moving without burning out.

This reflection is not an endpoint.

It's a handover.

You already know how to improvise.

The question now is how you adapt.

* * *

The laundry at Nanutarra Station. Where routine depended on preparation, and comfort only existed if you made it work.

* * *

Sleeping quarters at Nanutarra Station. Where rest was functional, privacy was minimal, and resilience was learned without being named.

* * *

My backyard at Nanutarra Station with Mount Murray in the distance (the "sleeping elephant"). Space was abundant, boundaries were few, and imagination had room to stretch.

* * *

Preparing for a BMX race in Karratha. Focus before the gate dropped, learning early that progress often comes from persistence rather than position.

* * *

Me with the Red Dog statue in Dampier, 1983. A story of loyalty and belonging that travelled the highway long before it reached the screen.

* * *

Supplier Course, RAAF Wagga, 1989. Learning the discipline behind the uniform, immediately after recruit training.

* * *

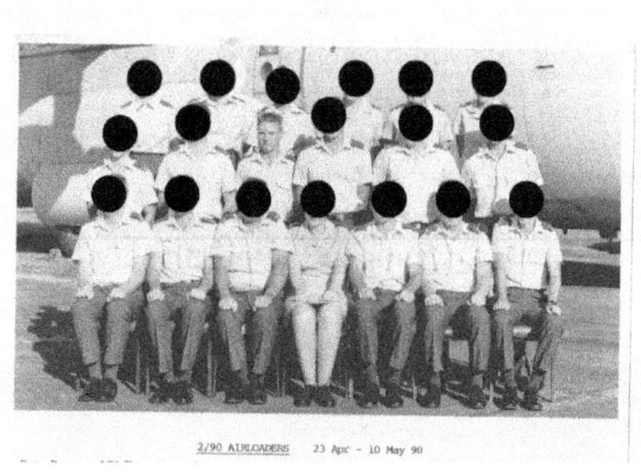

Aircraft Loaders Course, RAAF Richmond, 1990. Training where precision, discipline, and safety became non-negotiable.

* * *

Kenny Said So. A farewell cake from the CTEC team in Scottsdale, Arizona, marking the close of an ERP implementation. What began as guidance became shared judgement; a moment when decisions no longer needed me in the room.

* * *

5

End of Part One – Putting It to Work in Your Business

Improvise in Your Business

Improvisation is how most small and medium-sized businesses typically start; it's how they survive their first shocks. There comes a point where it's worth asking a different question: **where is improvisation still serving us, and where is it quietly holding us back?**

This section is an invitation to look at your own business through that lens. Not to judge, but to notice.

Where Improvisation is Helping

Start with what's working. Improvisation usually shows up in at least one of the following areas.

You can:

- Make decisions quickly when conditions change.

- Re-route work when a person, supplier, or system fails.
- Find ways to deliver for customers, even when the plan breaks.
- Try something new without a six-month approval process.

Take a moment and jot down three examples from the last six months where you or your team improvised well.

- What changed suddenly?
- What did you do?
- What was the outcome?

You don't need a template for this, a few bullet points are enough. The goal is simply to recognise that improvisation is already a strength, not a theoretical concept.

Where Improvisation is Becoming a Risk

Now look at the other side: improvisation becomes a liability when it is no longer an exception, but the only way things get done.

Some warning signs:

- The same problems keep reappearing, and every fix is a fresh improvisation.
- "Ask [name]" is the answer to most questions.
- You can't predict next month's workload without asking two or three key people what's "in their heads".
- New team members struggle because "how we do things here" is ingrained in habits, not in any simple guide.
- You feel uneasy about taking a real break, because too much

depends on you being reachable.

You don't need to fix all of this now. Simply circle the two or three that feel most familiar. That's where improvisation has done its job and is now asking for help from the next stage: adaptation.

A Few Questions For Owners and Leaders

Use these questions with a notebook, a leadership team, or even a trusted advisor:

- If I were absent from the business for four weeks, what would stall first?
- Where are we relying on individual heroics to get through each week?
- Which parts of our customer experience are consistent, and which depend on who picks up the phone?
- Where have we said, "That's just how it is," instead of asking, "Is there another way to achieve the outcome?"
- Where have we solved the same problem more than twice in different ways?

You may notice patterns. Often, they cluster around one or two areas: sales, delivery, cash flow, and people. That's useful information;it tells you where adaptation will have the greatest impact.

A Small Experiment, Not a Grand Plan

Before moving into the next part of this book, choose one area where you are currently improvising heavily and run a small experiment.

- Name the outcome clearly.
- Ask, "What's the simplest repeatable way we could do this next time?"
- Write that way down in half a page or less.
- Try it for the next three to five instances before it is changed again.

No policies. No manuals. Just a simple, shared way of doing something you've been making up each time.

If it works, keep it. If it doesn't, adjust it. Either way, you've begun to turn improvisation into something sturdier.

That's the bridge to the next stage.

Improvisation got you moving.

Adaptation will decide how far you can go.

II

Part Two

Adapt

Adaptation is what happens after improvisation. It is the point where experience is reflected on, lessons are absorbed, and deliberate change begins. This section explores how adjusting to new environments, roles, and realities builds resilience, relevance, and long-term capability in life and business.

6

When the environment changes

When Improvisation Is No Longer Enough

Improvisation gets you moving. Adaptation is what happens when movement becomes your new normal.

At some point, circumstances stop being temporary. The environment does not revert. The situation does not reset. What worked yesterday no longer works today, not because it was wrong, but because conditions have changed.

That is when adaptation begins.

Some of my earliest lessons in adaptation did not come from my own choices, but from watching my father navigate responsibility well beyond what his formal education suggested he should have been capable of.

My dad left high school early. Like many men of his generation, staying at school was not always an option or a priority. After a number of different jobs, he found himself working at Kanga Pet Meats in Osborne Park, Perth, Western Australia.

On paper, it was not a senior leadership role. In reality, it was substantial. By the 1970's, my father was effectively operating at the level of an operations manager, overseeing people, production, and performance in a business turning over around eleven million dollars a year. That was a serious responsibility, particularly for someone without formal qualifications, management training, or corporate backing.

What he had instead was judgement.

He understood how work actually got done. He understood people. He understood when something was not working and needed to change. He did not manage by theory. He managed by observing, adjusting, and learning as he went. That distinction matters.

Improvisation helps you find a way in. Adaptation is what allows you to stay there. This pattern repeated itself in our family life when we moved to Nanutarra Station.

This was not a short-term change or a novelty. It was a complete shift in environment, lifestyle, and expectations.

Life on the station removed convenience very quickly.

There was no town water. Our water came from a windmill. If the windmill was not turned on, there was no water. It was not something you assumed would be available. It was something you actively managed.

There was no electricity. The refrigerator ran on kerosene. Light at night came from gas lanterns. When the sun went down, the day largely ended unless you planned otherwise.

Hot water came from a hot water donkey.

If you did not light the donkey, there was no hot water. No shortcuts. No switch to flick. You learned quickly that comfort required preparation and effort.

The laundry was two cement troughs. There was no washing machine. All washing was done by hand. That meant time, labour, and prioritisation. You did not wash clothes on impulse. You planned for it.

We lived in corrugated iron shearers' quarters. They were practical, functional, and unforgiving in the heat. Comfort was secondary to utility.

And then there was the wildlife.

King Brown snakes and Spinifex snakes did not stay politely outside. They slithered through the kitchen. You learned to be aware of your environment at all times.

Skye, the retired racehorse, would poke his head through the kitchen door each morning, waiting patiently for his carrot, as if this were entirely normal behaviour.

This was not an adventure. This was daily life.

Adaptation here was not creative or clever. It was necessary. You learned routines that worked in that environment. You learned what mattered and what did not. You learned that if you did not take responsibility for the basics, the system failed immediately.

This is an important lesson for business leaders.

Many SME owners operate as though their business exists in an ideal environment. Reliable utilities. Stable supply.

Predictable labour. Consistent costs.

But real businesses operate much more like Nanutarra Station.

If you do not actively manage cash flow, it dries up.

If you do not invest effort into your systems, they fail.

If you do not plan, nothing works by default.

Adaptation is recognising the environment you are actually operating in and designing how the business works within it.

This became even clearer for me when I transitioned from the School of the Air to attending school in Karratha.

Academically, I was ahead. Roughly six months ahead of the curriculum.

And I made the classic mistake.

I assumed that meant I knew everything.

I stopped listening properly. I disengaged. I confused early advantage with competence.

The lesson arrived quickly and without ceremony.

Adaptation is not just about catching up. Sometimes it is about recalibrating your mindset when you think you are ahead.

In business, this shows up more often than people realise.

A business finds early success and assumes the formula will always work. Feedback gets ignored. Assumptions go unchallenged. Learning slows down.

Eventually, reality intervenes. Adaptation requires humility.

It requires recognising that past success does not guarantee future relevance. It requires staying curious even when things appear to be going well.

Returning to the classroom forced me to adapt socially and behaviourally, not just academically. Knowing the content was not enough. I had to learn how to learn in that environment. I had to adjust how I showed up.

That is a leadership lesson many business owners encounter later than they should.

As a business grows, the role of the owner changes. What worked when the business was small may actively hold it back as it scales. The habits that created momentum are not always the habits that create stability.

Adaptation is recognising when you need to change how you

lead, not just what you do.

This is where many SMEs struggle.

They are excellent at improvising. They solve problems quickly. They push through challenges. They make things work with limited resources.

What they do not always do is adapt structurally.

They keep decision-making centralised. They rely on personal heroics. Knowledge stays in people's heads rather than in processes. Growth feels risky because it threatens control.

Adaptation is what breaks that pattern.

It turns lived experience into capability.

It allows the business to function well even when the owner is not present. It replaces effort with intent, and chaos with rhythm.

Looking back, the thread running through my father's career, life on Nanutarra Station, and my return to formal schooling is clear. Adaptation was never theoretical.

It was practical. Grounded. Non-negotiable.

If you did not light the donkey, there was no hot water.

If you did not turn on the windmill, there was no water.

If you did not wash the clothes, they stayed dirty.

Cause and effect were immediate and unforgiving.

Business works the same way.

You cannot outsource responsibility for adaptation. You cannot wait for conditions to improve. You either adjust how you operate, or you absorb the consequences.

For SME owners, this chapter is an invitation to pause and reflect.

Where has your environment changed permanently?

What habits are you still using because they once worked?

What systems are missing because you have been compensating personally?

Adaptation begins when you answer those questions honestly. Improvisation gets you through the moment.

Adaptation ensures you are still standing and still growing when the moment does not pass.

And once adaptation is embedded, the focus can finally shift from coping to succeeding.

7

Reflection

Adapting to Your Real Environment

Take ten quiet minutes to reflect on the questions below. Write your answers down. Don't overthink them. Honesty matters more than polish.

What has changed permanently in your business?

Consider your market, customers, costs, team, or personal capacity. Identify one change that is not temporary, even if you've been treating it as such.

* * *

Where are you relying on personal effort instead of structure?

Think about areas where things only work because you are involved. Ask yourself what would fail if you stepped away for two weeks.

What "donkey" are you forgetting to light?

What basic activity, system, or routine must be done consistently for your business to function properly, but is currently being neglected or taken for granted?

What once worked well, but no longer fits your environment?

Identify one habit, process, or way of leading that helped in the past, but may now be limiting resilience or growth.

* * *

What is one deliberate adjustment you can make in the next 30 days?

Choose a single, practical change that improves how the business operates within its current reality. Keep it small. Make it intentional.

Adaptation is not about fixing everything at once.

It is about recognising reality and adjusting how you operate so effort turns into momentum — not exhaustion.

8

Learning the hard way

Adaptation Is Earned

If improvisation is the spark that gets you moving, adaptation is the grind that keeps you moving.

Improvisation can look clever from the outside. Adaptation rarely does. Adaptation is often slow, repetitive, uncomfortable and, at times, deeply frustrating. It is not the dramatic "breakthrough moment". It is the quiet, persistent work of becoming capable in a new reality.

After the surgery on my legs, I went through twelve months of physiotherapy to learn to walk again.

Not *walk better*.

Walk again.

That distinction matters because it reframes everything that follows. There are times in life when you are not improving a skill you already have. You are rebuilding the skill from the ground up, one uncomfortable repetition at a time.

Physiotherapy is not glamorous. It is stretching, balance

work, parallel bars, learning muscle memory, relearning posture, and recalibrating movement. It is the discomfort of being forced into positions your body resists. It is fatigue arriving faster than it should. It is frustration at not getting it the first time, or the second, or the tenth.

It is also humbling. As a kid, I wanted to do it on my own. I was determined to be self-sufficient. I wanted the independence — and the dignity — of proving to myself, and everyone else, that I could do it.

But part of adapting is learning when independence becomes stubbornness.

My parents' care and support were paramount to my success. They were there in the background, doing the practical things that made progress possible. Transport. Encouragement. Routine. Consistency. The steady presence that helps you keep going when motivation dips.

And yet, even with all that support, the work still fell to me. That's one of the clearest truths about adaptation.

Support helps, but it does not substitute. Encouragement matters, but it does not move the legs. Advice is useful, but it does not do the repetitions. At some point, you still have to step up and do the work.

This is where the business lesson begins.

In business, many owners and leaders want change, but what they really want is change without discomfort. They want a new outcome without a new behaviour. They want a different result without having to stretch, sweat, repeat, and feel awkward in the process.

It does not work that way.

Businesses, like bodies, develop habits. Those habits create patterns. Patterns create performance. When the environment changes, those patterns can start to fail — not because the people are failing, but because the old movement no longer fits the new conditions.

Adaptation is the willingness to be uncomfortable long enough to build a new pattern. In physiotherapy, you learn quickly that the first attempt is rarely good. You wobble. You tire. You get it wrong. You feel the limits of your current capacity. You discover where you compensate. You learn where you've been relying on one "strong" method that is now working against you.

In business, it is the same.

When you implement a new system, a new role, a new process, or a new expectation, you will wobble. Productivity may dip. People get tired. Mistakes appear. You feel like you are going backwards.

This is normal.

It is not a sign that the change is wrong. It is a sign that you are in the middle of adaptation.

One of the traps leaders fall into is assuming that discomfort equals failure. They panic when performance wobbles. They revert to old habits because it feels safer. They abandon the change before it has time to form muscle memory.

But growth requires a phase of awkwardness.

No one walks confidently on parallel bars on day one. You earn stability by staying with the work.

Adaptation demands patience, but not passive patience. It demands the kind of patience that keeps turning up.

That year of physiotherapy taught me something that people don't talk about enough. Adaptation involves vulnerability.

Vulnerability is not weakness. It is exposure. It is admitting that you cannot do what you used to do, or that you do not yet know how to do what you now must do. It is asking for help.

It is accepting guidance. It is being seen in the messy middle.

As a kid, that was hard. I wanted to be capable. I wanted to be independent. I wanted to get it right quickly.

But in rehabilitation, you learn that progress often comes from accepting support rather than resisting it.

That lesson is critical for SME owners.

Many business owners are highly self-sufficient people. They are used to coping. They are used to figuring things out. They carry responsibility. They are the ones others rely on.

That very strength can become the thing that blocks adaptation.

Because adaptation, especially in leadership, often requires you to say, "I can't do this alone anymore."

Not because you are incapable, but because the environment has changed. The business has grown. The stakes are higher. The complexity is greater. The old operating model is no longer sufficient.

A leader who can be appropriately vulnerable creates space for others to step up. They invite capability into the room.

This is what your business needs as it stabilises and grows. It needs you to shift from being the hero to being the designer. From being the fixer to being the builder. From being the one who carries everything to being the one who creates conditions where others can carry their part.

Around this time in our lives, my parents also had to adapt again — in a different way.

In 1980, we arrived in Karratha, and Dad secured a new job with Pilbara Harbour Services in 1983. The deal was simple:

Want the job? Take the house in Dampier, twenty kilometres down the road.

On the surface, this was not a dramatic change. It was still the Pilbara. Still the same rough edges and big skies. But any time you move house, you know it is never "small". It is a disruption.

New home. New routines. New community. New expectations. New social landscape.

It was adapting again, setting up again, settling in again.

This kind of repeated change teaches you something that is easy to underestimate.

Adaptation is not always one big pivot. Sometimes it is a series of smaller adjustments, stacked one after another, that slowly reshape who you are and how you operate.

In business, this is exactly how it happens.

A new client type comes in, and suddenly your service model needs adjustment.

A new hire arrives, and you have to change how you communicate.

A supplier changes terms, and you have to tighten cash flow rhythms.

A compliance requirement appears, and you need better documentation.

A team member leaves, and you have to reallocate responsibilities.

None of these changes alone might be life-altering. But together, they can change the business completely.

The question is whether you adapt intentionally, or whether you simply absorb change until you become reactive and fatigued.

My schooling years reflected this same pattern of intentional adaptation. I attended Karratha Senior High School from Years

8 to 11, and then I repeated Year 11 to improve my grades. That decision wasn't made because repeating a year is fun or socially comfortable. It was made for a purpose.

It was made to support my enlistment in the Australian Defence Force. Our family has a long history of military service. And if you were staying in Karratha or Dampier at that time, there weren't a lot of employment options outside the mines, Hamersley Iron, or Pilbara Harbour Services.

I had a different vision. I wanted to join the military as an electrical technician.

That meant I had to adapt again — but this time the adaptation was chosen, not forced. It was strategic.

Repeating Year 11 was not about pride. It was about positioning. It was a deliberate short-term sacrifice to create a longer-term opportunity.

This is an important business lesson.

Many SME owners chase progress that looks good in the short term but undermines the long term. They avoid temporary discomfort, even when that discomfort would build capability, credibility, or stability.

Sometimes the smartest move is the one that looks like a step back to those who don't understand the strategy.

Repeating Year 11 taught me that adaptation is often a decision to do the unglamorous work others won't do, because you can see where it leads.

That theme continued when I secured school-based work experience with Phillips Communications in Karratha, with the help of Mum and Dad.

This was practical, hands-on exposure, repairing two-way radios, installing base stations, installing antennas on vehicles and buildings. Doing real work, in real conditions, with real expectations.

It wasn't a paid gig in the usual sense. I didn't get cash. What I got was access to second-hand parts — and for me, that was gold.

Those parts, combined with my subscription to *Electronics Australia*, became my learning system. I used them to build, tinker, and stretch my capability. I made my own alarm clock. A motion sensor. A few other gadgets. Each one required reading, testing, failing, troubleshooting, and trying again.

That learning wasn't abstract. It was applied.

The result was that I excelled at Electronics as an elective subject in Year 11 — not because I was magically gifted, but because I had been building competency through repetition and curiosity.

Again, the business lesson is sitting right there.

Adaptation is not a motivational quote. It is a learning loop.

It is doing the work, receiving feedback from reality, adjusting, and trying again.

SMEs that adapt well tend to build learning loops into their operations, even informally. They run small experiments. They test offers. They refine messaging. They look at what customers respond to. They improve onboarding. They tighten delivery. They learn from mistakes without being crushed by them.

In contrast, businesses that struggle to adapt often treat learning as optional, or as something they'll do when things calm down.

But things rarely calm down. Not permanently.

So capability needs to be built while you move, not after you stop.

The two-way radio work also taught me about systems.

A radio doesn't care about your intention. It cares about inputs, configuration, signal, and environment. If you install an antenna poorly, performance suffers. If you don't ground something properly, you'll have problems. If you ignore interference and atmospheric conditions, you'll blame the device when the issue is the context.

In SMEs, leaders often run into the same trap. They blame people when the system is the issue. They blame attitude when the process is unclear. They blame motivation when expectations are fuzzy. They blame staff when the business has grown, but the operating model hasn't.

Technology work teaches you to ask a different question:

What is actually happening here?

What are the inputs?

What is the system designed to produce?

Where is the interference?

That mindset is pure adaptation. It's not emotional; it's practical. It's grounded in reality.

As my Defence ambition became more real, another adaptation was required. I needed to get my grades up in Mathematics 1 and Physics to support the completion of the entrance examinations for the Defence Force.

So we did what was needed.

Two years of tutoring. Repetition. Practice. Improvement.

It wasn't a quick fix. It was consistent work, sustained over time, until performance matched the requirement.

And that is one of the most commercially relevant lessons you can take from this chapter.

A lot of business owners want a quick answer to long-term problems.

They want better profit without changing pricing, delivery,

or cost control.

They want a better culture without changing leadership behaviour.

They want better sales without building a repeatable sales rhythm.

They want better staff retention without improving clarity, training, and workload design.

Those are not quick fixes, they are capability gaps.

Capability gaps are addressed the same way academic gaps are addressed: through learning, repetition, feedback, and time. This is what many leaders resist, especially those who are used to being competent.

It can feel uncomfortable to admit you have a gap. It can feel frustrating to be a beginner again. It can feel vulnerable to be coached, tutored, guided, or corrected.

But that vulnerability is often the doorway to growth.

In business, I've seen owners transform simply by accepting coaching, seeking feedback, and doing the repetition required to build a new skill.

Not because they were broken. Because they were adapting.

Which brings us back to a thread that runs through this entire chapter.

Adaptation is earned. It is earned in the physio room, one painful stretch at a time. It is earned in the move to a new town, one routine at a time. It is earned in repeating a school year, one improved grade at a time.

It is earned on the job, one repaired radio at a time.

When you look at it that way, adaptation stops feeling mysterious. It becomes a process.

And if it is a process, it can be led. This is good news for SME owners. Because it means you are not at the mercy of change.

You can develop the capacity to meet change.

All of these early experiences taught me the mechanics of adaptation before I had language for it. What I didn't yet understand was how those same principles would be tested later — not in school or study, but inside a complex organisation, where decisions carried real consequences for people, systems, and livelihoods.

Adapt — Learning to Outgrow Who I Was

I didn't arrive at adaptation through theory.

I arrived there through repetition.

When the Australian Defence Force made the decision to discontinue operating the Huey helicopter, my role at BAE Systems Australia came to a natural close. Like most people would, I began looking for what came next. That search led me, in March 2006, to a Logistics Officer role with TAE Aerospace, then known as Tasman Aviation Enterprises.

At the time, my world was relatively contained. I led a small team, many of whom were marking time while waiting for apprenticeship opportunities. The work was honest, structured, and familiar. I understood the environment, the expectations, and my place within it.

That sense of stability didn't last.

Within months, Tasman Aviation Enterprises merged with the former 501 Wing Engine Business Unit, bringing with it responsibility for the Pratt & Whitney TF30 engine that powered the F-111. Overnight, my team grew to ten. My scope expanded across Amberley and Brisbane Airport. My role shifted to Warehouse Group Leader.

It was my first clear lesson that adaptation rarely arrives with warning — and almost never waits for permission.

What followed over the next seventeen years was not a linear career, but a pattern.

The organisation evolved. Platforms entered service and retired. Names changed. Structures shifted. Each time, I was required to pause, reassess, and recalibrate — not just what I did, but how I thought about leadership.

As TAE's remit expanded to include deeper-level maintenance of the F404-400 engine supporting the F/A-18 Classic fleet, my team grew again. Responsibilities stretched across state borders. Later, internal reorganisations pulled procurement into my remit, growing my team to twenty. Then, with the retirement of the F-111 platform, the team contracted once more.

Expansion.

Contraction.

Redefinition.

By 2014, I found myself acting in the role of Materials, Manufacturing and Repair Manager, leading a team of around sixty people — many of them highly technical specialists. For the first time, success depended less on my grounding in supply chain and more on my ability to understand how engineers think, speak, and reason.

Adaptation, I learned, is not always about learning more.

Sometimes, it's about learning differently.

In 2015, I was seconded to the company's ERP implementation project, introducing IFS into the business. Following the successful go-live, I transitioned into the finance function — the system-owning department at the time — reporting directly to the CFO and managing external consultants responsible for delivering the system to specification.

It was another shift in identity. I was no longer operating primarily in operations. I was now working at the intersection of systems, governance, and financial accountability.

By 2019, when a dedicated IT department was established, I found myself adapting yet again — this time into technology. I became a subject matter expert across multiple system modules and warehouse automation solutions, learning SQL despite having once struggled to program a Commodore 64.

The irony wasn't lost on me.

Each transition was survivable. Some were energising. Others were uncomfortable.

All of them required me to let go of an identity that had once made me competent.

Then, in 2023, after seventeen years with the organisation, adaptation arrived without my consent.

I was made redundant.

For the first time since I started working at fourteen, continuity disappeared overnight. There was no gradual transition. No overlapping identity to step into. Just silence — and questions.

What followed was a period of uncertainty. Panic, if I'm honest. I did what many people do in that moment. I searched for the next role, driven by responsibility to my family and the practical realities of life.

What steadied me wasn't optimism. It was reflection.

Looking back across three decades of work, I could see a pattern I hadn't fully named before. I had spent my career helping organisations navigate complexity — adapting systems, structures, teams, and ways of thinking. What I hadn't done was formally articulate that capability.

That realisation led me to the Institute of Advisors, and ultimately to becoming a Certified Professional Business

Advisor.

It wasn't reinvention. It was recognition.

I wasn't becoming someone new. I was finally choosing to stand in the work I had been doing all along.

Adaptation, I came to understand, isn't about avoiding disruption. It's about deciding who you become after disruption removes who you were before.

When adaptation is understood as a process rather than a personality trait, leadership stops feeling reactive and starts becoming deliberate.

First, you acknowledge reality without denial. The parallel bars are what they are. The business environment is what it is. You stop wishing it were different and start responding to what's real.

Second, you commit to the repetitions. You build the new skill. You run the new rhythm. You practise the new conversation. You implement the new process. You keep turning up.

Third, you accept support without surrendering agency. You are still responsible. You still lead. But you stop insisting you must do it alone.

That is adaptation.

It is not dramatic. It is not instant. But it is powerful.

And if you are a business owner reading this, there is a good chance you are in the middle of it right now.

You may be rebuilding capacity after a tough season.

You may be adjusting to a changed market.

You may be learning to lead a bigger team.

You may be moving from informal operations into structured

delivery.

You may be trying to grow without burning out.

If so, take heart.

The discomfort doesn't mean you're failing. It may simply mean you're doing the work of adaptation.

And that work, over time, turns effort into capability. It turns coping into confidence. It turns change into progress.

9

Reflection

The Adaptation Loop

Take ten minutes and answer these honestly.

Where are you currently on the parallel bars?

What area of your business feels awkward, tiring, or unstable because you're learning a new way of operating?

***

What are you still trying to do on your own that now requires support?

Support might be a coach, a mentor, a team member stepping up, or a system that reduces reliance on you.

What capability gap needs repetition, not motivation?

Choose one area — sales rhythm, pricing confidence, delegation, cash-flow discipline, or leadership conversations — where consistency matters more than effort.

What simple practice can you commit to for the next 30 days?

Not a complete overhaul. One routine. One behaviour that builds stability through repetition.

* * *

What is one deliberate adjustment you can make this week to reduce fragility?

Think structure, clarity, or support — not heroics.

70

Adaptation is not dramatic.

It is earned through repetition, supported by structure, and strengthened over time.

10

Choosing a different path

Adapting When the Plan Breaks

By the time I reached the Defence Force recruitment process, I believed I had done everything right.

As covered in the previous chapter, I repeated Year 11. I had undergone tutoring in Mathematics and Physics. I had put in the work. The goal was clear: enlist in the Australian Defence Force as an electrical technician.

This was not a vague ambition. It was deliberate — the result of years of thought, family discussion, and preparation

So, when the invitation to attend the Australian Defence Force Recruitment process arrived, it felt like validation. All the effort had been worth it. The logistics alone made it feel significant.

I was sixteen years old, living in Karratha, and I was flown to Perth for testing. I had never been on an aeroplane before. Boarding the aircraft for the one-and-a-half-hour flight was both exciting and intimidating. It was new territory in every sense.

I remember clutching my schoolwork, doing last-minute revision as the aircraft climbed out of Karratha. Looking back, it was probably more about managing nerves than genuinely improving performance, but it felt important at the time. That feeling is familiar to anyone stepping into a high-stakes situation.

You prepare. You revise. You rehearse. You tell yourself that preparation will carry you through. Sometimes it does.

Sometimes it doesn't.

On the day of the exams, we were ushered into a room filled with others in the same position. Different backgrounds. Different ambitions. Same nerves.

What I hadn't expected was the structure of the process.

The testing was run in a round-robin format. Each stage acted as a filter. Those who did not meet the required standard at each stage were called out of the room.

There was no gentle easing into it. You either progressed or you didn't. This was my first exposure to an environment where outcomes were binary and public. You stayed, or you were removed.

I adapted quickly.

Rather than fixating on the room thinning out, I chose to focus on each exam on its own merits. One test at a time. One hurdle at a time. No catastrophising.

That ability to compartmentalise would become important later in my career. Then came the moment I had been training for... Mathematics and Physics.

I opened the paper and worked methodically through the questions. Addition. Subtraction. Multiplication. Division.

Algebra. Geometry.

I remember feeling a surge of confidence as I moved through the basics. And then, with genuine excitement, I reached the Mathematics 1 and Physics questions.

This was the good stuff. The material I had worked hard to master. The part that aligned with my goal.

The exam finished. We waited.

And then my name was called.

I was devastated.

I was advised that my scores were not satisfactory for the electrical technician role. The reason stunned me.

I had failed the addition and subtraction section.

In my eagerness to get to the advanced material, I had rushed through the fundamentals. I had assumed they were a given. They weren't.

In that moment, I was convinced my career was over before it had even begun. Years of effort, undone by something so basic. This is one of the most important adaptation lessons of my life.

Competence in advanced areas does not excuse weakness in the fundamentals. That lesson applies everywhere.

In business, leaders often rush to strategy, growth, innovation, or optimisation while neglecting the basics. Cash flow discipline. Clear roles. Simple processes. Communication. Customer service.

They want to get to the good stuff. But the fundamentals still count. Often more than anything else.

What happened next changed the trajectory of my life.

The examiner then advised my mum and me that while I hadn't qualified for an electrical technician, I had successfully met the entry requirements for several other roles.

The list was longer than I expected.

RAAF Police.

Police Dog Handler.

Physical Training Instructor.

Cook.

Cook's Assistant.

Musician.

Supplier.

Clerk Supply.

I had never been offered so many options at once.

At sixteen, I reacted exactly as you'd expect.

RAAF Police? Not eligible. Too young.

Police Dog Handler? Same problem.

Physical Training Instructor? Again, age.

Musician? I can't even play the triangle.

Cook or Cook's Assistant? Not for me.

Clerk? Absolutely not.

Then there was "Supplier".

"What's a supplier?" I asked.

I was told it was essentially a storeman role. I thought about it for all of ten seconds. I worked at Dampier Woolworths after school and on weekends. I stocked shelves. I handled inventory. I dealt with customers. I managed stock movement.

"How hard can it be to put something in a box and put it on a shelf?" I said — with the confidence only a sixteen-year-old can have."

And just like that, the plan changed.

I completed the initial paperwork, began the enlistment process, and flew home to Dampier. In July 1988, I left school. Another decision with long-term consequences, as my formal education record now only shows completion of Year 10. At the time, it felt practical. I worked at Woolworths until my enlistment date of 4 January 1989.

This chapter could easily be framed as a story about failure or missed opportunity. It isn't. It's a story about adaptation when the original plan breaks. This is where many people get stuck. They build a plan. They invest emotionally in that plan. They tie their identity to that plan.

And when reality intervenes, they either freeze or walk away. Adaptation requires a different response.

It requires separating the goal from the method.

My goal was not "be an electrical technician".

My goal was to join the Defence Force and build a career.

Once I re-framed that, options appeared.

This is a critical business lesson. Many SME owners confuse their *first idea* with their *actual objective*.

They become attached to a product, a service, a market, or a role because that's how they imagined success would look. When the market pushes back, instead of adapting, they dig in. Adaptation asks a different question.

"What am I really trying to achieve here?"

Once you answer that honestly, methods become flexible.

The supplier role became my entry point. It wasn't glamorous. It wasn't the original plan. But it aligned with my skills, my experience, and my immediate eligibility.

And it opened doors.

This is another place where adaptation often clashes with ego. At sixteen, I didn't have the maturity to articulate it, but I instinctively understood something important.

Momentum matters more than prestige.

Getting in mattered more than getting the "perfect" role.

In business, the same principle applies. Sometimes the best

move is not the one that looks impressive. It's the one that gets you inside the system, learning, contributing, and building credibility.

The Defence Force, like many large organisations, rewards competence, reliability, and adaptability over time. Entry point matters less than performance once you're in.

That lesson would repeat itself later in my civilian career.

There's another subtle but powerful lesson in this chapter.

The exam process didn't just test knowledge. It tested composure, prioritisation, and attention to basics under pressure.

I didn't fail because I didn't know the material.

I failed because I misjudged what mattered most in that moment. In business, this shows up constantly.

Leaders under pressure skip basics.

They stop communicating clearly.

They rush decisions.

They assume foundations are solid because they once were. Pressure doesn't just reveal gaps in knowledge. It reveals gaps in discipline. Adaptation is learning how you behave under pressure and adjusting accordingly.

That experience also highlighted the importance of feedback. The examiner didn't simply say "no". They explained why. They showed me where I'd missed, and they presented alternatives.

In business, good feedback is often the difference between stagnation and adaptation. Unfortunately, many business owners operate in poor feedback environments. Customers leave quietly. Staff disengage silently. Financial signals are ignored until they become urgent.

Adaptation improves dramatically when feedback is welcomed early. The earlier you receive it, the cheaper it is to act on.

Looking back, leaving school early was another adaptation that carried unintended consequences. At the time, it made sense. I had a job. I had an enlistment date. I was focused on the next step.

What I didn't fully appreciate was how long formal records follow you. That's another important lesson for leaders.

Short-term decisions often have long-term echoes.

Adaptation doesn't mean acting without consequence. It means acting with awareness. You don't always get a perfect view of the future, but you can pause long enough to ask, "What might this close off later?"

In business, this applies to pricing decisions, contracts, hiring, systems, and governance. What feels efficient now may limit flexibility later.

Adaptation includes learning to think beyond the immediate horizon. Despite the missed steps, the outcome mattered.

I enlisted on 4 January 1989.

What began as a compromised plan became a career foundation. And that's perhaps the most reassuring lesson for anyone reading this. You do not need a perfect start.

You need responsiveness, humility, and the willingness to adjust. Adaptation is not about getting everything right.

It's about staying in the game long enough to learn.

For SME owners, this chapter holds several practical insights:

- Fundamentals matter more under pressure, not less.
- Advanced capability does not excuse weak basics.
- Feedback is a gift, even when it's uncomfortable.
- Momentum often matters more than prestige.
- Plans are tools, not identities.

Adaptation is what allows you to recover when the plan breaks without abandoning the goal.

As we move into the next chapter, the focus shifts again.

From adapting to enter the system, to adapting within it.

From individual effort to responsibility for others.

From learning to follow structure to learning how to lead.

And that, as it turns out, requires a whole new kind of adaptation.

11

Reflection

Take a few minutes to consider the questions below. Write your responses down, even briefly.

What goal are you currently attached to, rather than the outcome it serves?

Where might flexibility in the method create new options without abandoning the objective?

***

Which fundamentals are you assuming are "good enough"?

Under pressure, what basics might you be rushing past because you're focused on more advanced or interesting work?

Where has feedback already been given, but not fully absorbed?

This could be from customers, staff, advisors, or the numbers. What is it really telling you?

What opportunity could provide momentum, even if it isn't the ideal option?

Is there an entry point, partnership, role, or project that moves you forward while you build capability?

* * *

What short-term decision might limit future flexibility if left unexamined?

What would change if you paused long enough to consider its longer-term impact?

Adaptation is not abandoning the goal. It is choosing a better path when the original one closes.

12

Becoming someone others follow

New Rules, New Me

After qualifying for entry and completing the paperwork, the enlistment date was set for **4 January 1989.** That date was circled in my mind long before it arrived.

Mum, Dad and I drove down from Dampier to Perth. We spent Christmas with my sister, then stayed in Perth city the night before I had to report to the recruiting centre. Driving from the Pilbara to Perth was nothing new for the Newton family. From Nanutarra to Perth was roughly eighteen hours by car, longer again if you were starting from Dampier.. You don't "pop down" to Perth. You commit.

We were in an old blue **Ford Falcon 500 station wagon**, the kind with the fold-out rear window winder that sat flat with the exterior of the tailgate. Not much radio coverage out there, so we relied on cassettes. One album in particular became the soundtrack of that drive: *Be Happy '88*, with Bobby McFerrin singing, "Don't Worry, Be Happy".

That song has a way of testing you on a long trip.

It might have been comforting if it wasn't on repeat. Dad's singing didn't help either.

The night before enlistment, the nerves finally caught up with me. I wasn't a kid anymore, I wasn't an adult yet either. I was standing on the edge of a life I wanted, and that life was about to demand a different version of me.

On the morning of 4 January, we walked to the recruitment centre. Suitcase in hand. Mum and Dad are on either side of me.

They were anxious too, even if they tried to hide it.

Then came the oath. We stood, raised our right hand, and recited it. Even now, I hold that moment near and dear. It wasn't a formality. It felt like a line in the sand. A commitment. A decision that mattered.

And then it was time to say goodbye. That was the part I hadn't rehearsed.

My first time leaving for another state. South Australia. A life away from home. As Mum and Dad walked away, I felt a mix of pride, fear, excitement and a tightening in my chest that made it hard to breathe.

I wasn't just changing location. I was changing identity.

That is adaptation in its purest form. Not adjusting a process. Adjusting who you are.

The first big adaptation is always the same

Landing at Adelaide Airport and heading by bus to RAAF Base Edinburgh, it hit me quickly.

New clothes. New rules. New people. New routines. New

expectations. New me.

The military has a way of removing ambiguity. There is a standard for everything. How you dress. How you speak. How you move. How to make your bed. How to stand. How to learn.

If you are used to independence, that can feel suffocating.

If you are used to chaos, it can feel comforting.

For me, it was both.

There's a business lesson here that SME owners often miss.

Many people say they want structure, but what they really want is structure that doesn't challenge their habits. They want systems, but only if they feel natural on day one. They want new routines, but without the discomfort of being a beginner again.

Structure always feels uncomfortable at first, because it exposes inconsistency.

In the military, inconsistency is not tolerated for long. That might sound harsh, but it creates a powerful outcome. You stop relying on motivation and start relying on standards.

And standards, when applied properly, create repeatable performance.

That lesson translates directly to business. In small and medium enterprises, performance often depends on personalities. The business works because certain people know what to do. They carry knowledge in their heads and fill gaps with effort.This can work for a while.

But when the business grows, or the environment changes, effort becomes fragile. Standards and systems become essential.

The military taught me early that structure isn't there to restrict you. Done well, it's there to enable you.

Graduation and the reality of transition

Recruit training ended, and we prepared for graduation. I was excited and also disappointed. I hoped Mum and Dad could come and watch me "pass out". Not fainting. Graduation parade.

Two days before the ceremony, I found out Mum was coming. I was so happy. Proud. I wanted to show her I had made it through. I wanted her to see that the nervous kid who could hardly breathe on day one had pushed through and earned the next step.

After the parade, we received our next posting orders.

New South Wales, specifically Wagga Wagga.

I remember thinking, "And I thought Western Australia had strange names." I was headed to what is now known as RAAFSALT for school for administration and logistics training. What struck me most wasn't the location; it was the timing. I had only just made friends at Edinburgh, and now I was leaving them.

Transition again. The military trains you in adaptation by making it constant. Just as you settle, you move.

That's not a bad metaphor for business growth.

In SMEs, the moment you stabilise one part of the business, another part starts demanding attention. You fix delivery, then sales need structure. You stabilise sales, then staffing becomes the issue. You hire, then culture and leadership become the focus.

Constant transition is not a sign that the business is broken.

It is a sign the business is alive.

Here's the part that made me laugh: when we moved to Nanutarra, it was during the first term of Grade 5. I had a small band of friends I had to leave behind. One of them was

Michael.

Imagine my surprise when Michael, who had joined the RAAF on the same day as me, was on the same recruit course and was posted to the same supplier training course.

In a world where everything felt unfamiliar, one familiar face mattered.

That's another leadership lesson.

Adaptation is easier when you have anchors. A mentor. A mate. A supportive family member. A colleague who understands the context. In business, this is why peer networks, advisory relationships, and trusted sounding boards matter. Not because you need someone to do the work for you, but because transition is less isolating when you're not navigating it alone.

Learning what "Supplier" really means

We finished training at Wagga, and I was posted to RAAF Pearce, specifically Base Squadron, to work in the main warehouse.

Again: moving alone, new people, new work area. My first official posting. My first experience living in a dormitory.

I had entered the RAAF thinking "supplier" was basically storeman work. Put things in boxes, put them on shelves.

I quickly learned it wasn't that simple.

A supply function is a system. It is accountability, readiness, traceability, governance, and service. It sits behind operations and enables them. When it's done well, no one notices. When it's done poorly, everything suffers.

In aviation and Defence, supply isn't about convenience. It's about capability. If an aircraft is grounded because a part isn't available, it's not an inconvenience. It's a readiness issue.

That's when I first began to understand business systems properly. Not in a textbook sense. In a practical sense.

A business system is not paperwork. It's the invisible structure that makes performance repeatable. For SMEs, this is a critical shift.

Most small businesses start as effort-driven. "We'll make it work." The owner knows everything. The team asks the owner. Work gets done through relationships and memory.

But as you grow, memory becomes a risk. The business needs a system.

A system is simply a reliable way of doing something, so you don't have to reinvent it every time.

That's what I learned at Pearce.

I rotated through different postings: Hazardous Goods Store, Fuel Farm, Catering Section, the base gym, and then into Number 2 Flying Training School.

Each move required adaptation. New supervisors. New expectations. New standards. Different stakeholders. Different tempo.

And somewhere in that rotation, my passion for aviation and business systems became obvious, even if I couldn't articulate it fully at the time. I could see how the parts fit together. How decisions in one area created consequences in another. How standards improved performance. How clarity reduced rework.

that's the kind of thinking that has been valuable in every civilian role I've held.

Life changes that force leadership growth

Life did not stay neatly contained in uniform postings.

I married my wife. I welcomed her son as my own. I was discharged from the RAAF and began my civilian career.

In one sense, I simply changed suits. From RAAF uniform to civilian clothing. Doing essentially the same type of supply work, because it had been outsourced to civilian contractors, Airflite Pty. Ltd., but culturally, it was a different world.

In the RAAF, particularly during that era, many senior personnel were men of a certain vintage, and leadership was often blunt. "Do as I say" was common. Workplace equality and modern leadership expectations weren't what they are today.

Then I stepped into my first team outside the RAAF.

Seven women.

If I didn't adapt quickly — and I mean quickly — I wouldn't have lasted.

The technical work was not the challenge. The supply and equipment side was familiar. The challenge was me.

I was a new leader in a new culture, and I needed to shift my thinking fast. This is where people misunderstand leadership adaptation.

They think it's about learning policies and procedures.

It's not. Leadership adaptation is learning how your behaviour lands on other people. It's learning that competence doesn't automatically create trust.

It's learning that direction without respect becomes resistance.

And it's learning that if you want performance, you must create an environment where people can perform.

Around this time, I began to understand leadership development as layers.

Different models describe this differently, but one practical way of thinking about it is moving from **leading yourself**, to **leading others**, to **leading leaders**, and then to **leading through systems**.

When I was younger, I thought leadership was simply being in charge. Then I learned the hard way that being in charge is the smallest part of it.

The first level is always leading yourself. Your discipline. Your emotional regulation. Your consistency. Your integrity. People watch that more than they listen to your words.

Then comes leading others. Communication, expectations, feedback, coaching, conflict. If you avoid hard conversations, culture forms without you.

Then leading the leaders. Developing capability in others, so you're not the bottleneck.

Then leading through systems. The point at which the business can perform without constant intervention.

That shift from uniform to civilian leadership forced me into this learning curve at speed.

And it required vulnerability.

The kind that says: "I'm learning. Help me get this right."

One of the team members from that first civilian team is still a good friend to this day.

Hi Jacke.

That friendship is a reminder of something that often gets lost in leadership conversations. Leadership isn't about being the toughest person in the room. It's about being trustworthy.

And trust is built through respect, consistency, fairness, and the willingness to learn.

The bridge from Adapt to Succeed

Looking back, this entire sequence, enlistment, recruit training, postings, transitions, discharge, civilian leadership, it was adaptation after adaptation.

New environments. New rules. New expectations. New identity. New responsibilities. And here is the key point:

Adaptation is not the end goal.

Adaptation is the capability that allows you to move toward success without breaking.

In business, adaptation stabilises you. It helps you stay relevant. It prevents you from being crushed by change.

But at some stage, adaptation must become ownership.

That is where the next section begins, because succeeding is not just coping well. Succeeding is owning outcomes. It is choosing a direction, aligning people, building systems, and delivering results with intent.

Adaptation taught me how to function in new environments. Success would require something more.

It would require learning how to lead, how to build, and how to make performance repeatable, not by pushing harder, but by operating smarter.

And that is where we go next.

13

End of Part Two – Putting Adaptation to Work

Adaptation is what happens after the initial improvisation. The environment has changed. The rules are different. What got you moving now needs to become repeatable, not a one-off fix.

This section invites you to look at your business through an adaptation lens. Not to overhaul everything, but to notice where change has settled in and where you're ready to build on it.

Where Adaptation is Already Happening

Look for these signs first. Adaptation shows up when:

- You've stopped firefighting the same issues month after month.
- Your team can handle routine changes without escalating them to you.
- Cash flow, delivery, and customer work feel more pre-

dictable than they did six months ago.
- You've simplified something that used to take too much effort or too many people.

Jot down two or three examples from your business over the last year.

- What changed in your environment?
- How did you respond?
- What stayed stable as a result?

No need for long analysis, just note what worked. Adaptation often feels quiet because it's no longer dramatic—it's just how things are now.

Where Adaptation is Still Needed

Now scan for gaps. Adaptation lags when change demands fresh improvisation instead of settling into a rhythm.
Common signals:

- You're still the only person who knows how key decisions get made.
- Processes work for today's volume, but would break at 20% more.
- Team members ask the same "how do we handle X?" questions.
- You hesitate to delegate because "they won't do it the way I would."
- One person's absence creates a visible gap in momentum or output.

Circle the two that hit closest to home. Those are your leverage points—where small, deliberate adjustments will create the most stability.

Questions For Leaders and Teams

Use these solo, in a leadership huddle, or with a trusted advisor:

- What three environmental changes (market, team, costs, rules) have we introduced well?
- Where are we still reacting instead of responding from a stronger base?
- If we had to write down "how we do [key activity]" on one page, what would be missing?
- Which routines from six months ago no longer fit "who we are now"?
- Where does progress still feel like it depends on effort rather than design?

Patterns will surface. They often live in delivery, people decisions, or customer commitments. That's where adaptation does its deepest work.

One Experiment to Stabilise

Pick one area where adaptation is lagging. Run this simple test over the next four weeks:

- Name the outcome you want (e.g., "handle new quotes without me reviewing").
- List the three or four essential steps that always work.

- Write them down where the team can see — email, white-board, Microsoft Teams shared page.
- Ask the team to follow it for the next five instances and note what needs adjusting.

No big roll out. No training sessions. Just capture what's already working and test if others can run with it.

If it holds, you've adapted. If it doesn't, you've learned something. Either way, you're no longer fully improvising.

That's adaptation's gift.

It turns survival into something sustainable.

Improvisation got you moving. Adaptation keeps you steady. Now let's see what success looks like when it matures.

III

Part Three

SUCCEED

To succeed is to turn intent into outcome. It is the act of taking ownership, making deliberate decisions, and delivering results over time. This section explores how leaders convert improvisation and adaptation into consistent execution and outcomes that matter.

<h1 style="text-align:center">14</h1>

Unconscious leadership

Unconscious Leadership & Owning Outcomes

As outlined at the beginning of this section, to succeed is to achieve a desired outcome. By most measures, I had done exactly that. I was married. I had become a father of two. I had completed my career in the Royal Australian Air Force. I had also secured my first civilian role outside of the military.

On paper, I was succeeding. What I hadn't yet learned was how quietly success can create blind spots.

In reality, I was about to relearn almost everything.

While the uniform had changed, the environment had not yet caught up. My teachers and mentors in the military had largely been men of a certain vintage, operating in a time when leadership was primarily directive. Clear orders, clear hierarchy, clear compliance. That model worked in that context, and it had shaped how I understood leadership.

Civilian life challenged that understanding immediately.

As previously mentioned, my first team outside the military

consisted of seven women. While they were familiar with Defence life through spouses and exposure, they were not members of the military. They were professionals in their own right, with private-sector experience, expectations, and perspectives that did not fit neatly into the leadership model I had learned. What worked before did not work here.

I needed to reassess how I approached people. How I engaged. How I was motivated. How I recognised effort and contribution.

Civilian leadership challenged my assumptions immediately. What had worked in uniform no longer landed the same way. I wasn't failing, but I was operating with blind spots I couldn't yet see — and that realisation marked the true beginning of succeeding.

I quickly realised that being the subject matter expert only took you so far.

From a technical perspective, the aircraft technicians were well supported. Supply processes were sound. Equipment availability was managed. I was confident providing technical information and process guidance in a no-nonsense, matter-of-fact style. That approach had worked well in the military.

But dealing with people was different.

Nurturing people. Growing people. Understanding what motivated them, how they interpreted tone, and how my behaviour landed. In that space, I was out of my depth and drowning quickly.

At the time, the internet was still in its infancy. There was no instant access to leadership podcasts, blogs, or online courses. I relied on encyclopedias, libraries, magazines, periodicals, textbooks, and, most importantly, mentors and my parents.

What became clear was how little awareness I had of how

differently people absorb information, feedback, and tone.

Once again, I found myself back on my virtual parallel bars — relearning how to speak, listen, and adapt my language, not just my intent.

This time, the muscles I was stretching weren't in my legs.

They were in my mind.

That realisation crystallised one afternoon when I was pulled aside by the Operations Manager. He was a former senior member of Number 2 Flying Training School, someone I respected deeply. His feedback was calm, direct, and uncomfortable.

He told me, plainly, that my approach and mannerisms were not conducive to building a strong team.

There was no accusation in his tone. No judgement; just truth.

In that moment, I had a choice. I could defend my technical competence, remind myself that the work was getting done, and dismiss the feedback as soft. Or I could recognise that success at this level required something different.

So, I started walking again.

Slowly. Awkwardly. Consciously.

I began to observe how people responded to different styles of communication. I paid attention to when engagement increased or shut down. I learned when to speak and when to listen. When to direct and when to ask. When silence was more effective than instruction.

At first, everything felt forced. Conversations required effort. Praise felt unnatural. Feedback felt clumsy. I had to think about every interaction. Nothing was instinctive.

But over time, something shifted.

Without realising it at first, new habits began to form. I adjusted my tone without thinking. I asked better questions.

I paused before reacting. Trust started to build, not because I demanded it, but because consistency made it safe.

That was the moment leadership stopped being something I did, and started to become something I embodied.

As I've said, giving feedback felt clumsy, and receiving feedback was often brutal. One piece of feedback in particular landed hard. I was told that I did everything myself and, in doing so, I was preventing the team from assisting, learning, or taking ownership. At the time, it was confronting. I prided myself on being capable, reliable, and effective.

What I hadn't recognised was that my competence had become a constraint. I knew what I knew. But I still didn't know what I didn't know.

Letting go was difficult. It felt risky. It felt inefficient. It felt like losing control. Yet something unexpected happened once I began teaching, guiding, and supporting rather than doing.

The team stepped up.

They began to take ownership and responsibility. They learned when to ask questions and when to solve problems themselves. They showed interest in learning other parts of the role, not just their assigned tasks. Capability began to spread rather than bottleneck.

I was genuinely amazed.

Amazed that I had learned a new skill.

Amazed at how quickly the team grew.

And amazed at how much I enjoyed nurturing people.

That enjoyment surprised me most of all.

Somewhere in that process, I crossed an invisible line. I

had moved from being unaware of my limitations to being conscious of them. I could see the gaps. I could name them.

And, importantly, I could work on them.

I had progressed to knowing what I didn't know.

Around this time, another familiar framework resurfaced in my thinking. Those who remember quality assurance practices from the 1980's may recall the concept of continuous improvement, often described through the Plan–Do–Check–Act cycle, attributed to Edward Deming.

Without realising it, I had begun applying that same discipline to my leadership.

I would reflect on an interaction or situation and consider what I wanted to achieve (Plan). I would try a different approach (Do). I would observe the response and outcomes (Check). And then I would adjust accordingly (Act).

It wasn't elegant. It wasn't quick. But it worked.

More importantly, it gave me a way to learn deliberately rather than react emotionally. Leadership stopped being something that "just happened" and became something I could review, refine, and improve.

This learning loop has stayed with me ever since. I still use it today. And I use it with clients who are trying to grow beyond their current level of leadership. Because success is rarely about getting it right the first time.

It is about having a way to learn when you don't. The business lesson here is that many SME owners think they are still operators when, in fact, they have already become leaders. That mismatch creates friction. The business continues to rely on their effort instead of their direction, and progress depends on how much they personally can carry.

Over time, I stopped thinking so hard about how to lead.

Not because leadership had become easy, but because the repetition had done its work. The questions I once had to consciously ask began answering themselves. The behaviours I once rehearsed became instinctive. I noticed problems earlier. I responded more calmly. I trusted the process instead of rushing to fix everything myself.

Without realising it, leadership was becoming a habit.

When Leadership Stops Feeling Loud

Unconscious competence shows up most clearly under pressure. It always feels strange when you realise you've done something without thinking about it. Almost unsettling. One moment you're acting, the next you're wondering how it happened so smoothly.

Think back to when you first learned to ride a bike. In the beginning, everything required conscious effort. Sitting upright. Turning your knees inward to stabilise yourself. Pushing off with your dominant foot. Pressing down on the pedal with the other foot. Steering in the direction you wanted to go. Lift your foot onto the second pedal. Then synchronising balance, pedalling, and steering, all while trying not to fall off.

You couldn't hold a conversation while riding.

Or think about learning to drive a manual car. Steering in the direction of travel. Foot off the accelerator. Foot onto the clutch. Changing gears with your left hand. Slowly releasing the clutch while bringing the accelerator back in, all without stalling the car or veering off the road.

At first, every movement demanded attention. You couldn't talk while driving. You were too busy thinking. Leadership is no different.

In the early stages, I was consciously thinking about every interaction. Before a conversation, I would mentally rehearse, breathe, be aware of my tone of voice, be clear about what I wanted to say or teach, ensure the other person understood what I was saying, and make them comfortable enough to ask questions. All of this while maintaining eye contact, staying on topic, and delivering against the desired outcome of the conversation, task, or teaching moment.

It was mentally taxing.

Leadership felt like spinning plates, and dropping one meant losing momentum or trust. Then something shifted.

I remember attending a Myers-Briggs personality session focused on leadership styles. We completed the assessment, and the facilitator asked each person to share their dominant trait. When it was my turn, my results showed a strong split between supporting and nurturing.

The facilitator immediately told me I must have completed the assessment incorrectly. According to him, I should have had one clear, dominant style.

Without thinking, I replied, "Have you ever managed a team of seven women?"

The room went quiet.

In that moment, I realised something important. I hadn't consciously chosen those behaviours. I hadn't sat down and decided to lead that way. I had adapted. Learned. Practised.

And over time, those responses had become natural.

The point I'm making is this: with enough practice, things stop feeling deliberate.

You're not conscious of knowing how to do something — you just do it. The realisation usually comes after the fact. You're asked a question. A situation unfolds. A difficult conversation arises. And instead of freezing or overthinking, you respond. Calmly. Appropriately. Effectively. Everything flows.

That's unconscious competence.

It doesn't mean you stop learning. It means the fundamentals are now embedded. Pressure no longer triggers panic. It triggers presence. Your focus shifts from yourself to the situation in front of you.

Leadership, at this stage, becomes quieter. Less performative. More grounded. You're no longer trying to *be* a leader; you're simply leading.

And often, you don't even realise you're doing it until someone points it out.

When People Trusted the System, Not Just Me

This conscious–unconscious shift delivered benefits I hadn't even imagined.

The team began to relax. Not in a complacent way, but in a confident one. They felt empowered to perform their roles, achieve the required outcomes, and keep aircraft flying at Number 2 Flying Training School while RAAF student pilots focused on learning. Morale improved. People wanted to come to work.

And the work flowed.

Systems no longer felt forced. They simply became *how things were done*. Each team member could see how their role both depended on and supported others. Daily activities were no longer isolated tasks, but visible contributors to a larger outcome. The connection between effort and impact was clear.

Things started to click.

Things started to happen.

One of the moments I'm most proud of was when the team began offering their own ideas for improvement. Not because they were told to, but because they could see opportunities clearly. Suggestions came forward to redesign the front-store layout to better support parts being returned in a logical flow. Pick-up points for the base supply driver were rethought to reduce congestion. Tools requiring calibration and repair were clearly segregated to improve compliance and turnaround time.

These weren't small tweaks.

They were signals.

Signals that the team understood the system.

Signals that ownership had taken root.

Signals that leadership no longer depended solely on me.

Those moments made me proud — not of myself, but of what the team had become.

With that shift came something unexpected: relief.

As the team grew in confidence and capability, my stress reduced. I no longer felt compelled to be everywhere, approve everything, or fix every issue personally. I could step back and focus on working *on* the business rather than *in* it.

That meant engaging more effectively with the System Program Office, strengthening relationships with suppliers and customers, and thinking ahead rather than constantly reacting. Aircraft availability improved. Outcomes became more consistent. And most importantly, the environment became one where people grew, including me.

The business lesson here is simple, but profound: success begins when the organisation performs even when the leader steps back.

When trust shifts from the individual to the system, leadership becomes scalable. Stress reduces. Capability multiplies.

And results stop depending on how hard one person can push. That's not loss of control.

That's success taking hold.

The Quiet Power of Consistency, Letting Go, and Identity

The changes within the team and the changes within myself created something better than short-term business success.

They created consistency.

Processes and interactions began happening organically, yet they were structured, purposeful, and increasingly effortless. We moved from being reactive to proactive. Instead of responding to issues as they arose, we were planning ahead and pre-positioning for the anticipated needs of the team and our customers.

Tasks and actions became predictable. Not rigid, but sustainable.

And when pressure did arrive — a grounded aircraft, a team member unexpectedly absent — the systems and processes absorbed the impact. Work continued. Outcomes were delivered. The operation held steady.

It became boring, really.

But boring in the best possible way.

That was a lesson in itself. Intensity had once felt like leadership. Being busy. Being everywhere. Being needed. Consistency taught me something different. Steady performance outperformed bursts of effort every time. Sustainability didn't come from working harder; it came from

working more deliberately.

One of the steepest learning curves for me — and one I see

repeatedly with SME owners — was learning how to let go.

The business unit, like many small businesses, felt personal. It was something I had helped shape, something I cared deeply about. The temptation was to stay involved in every step, every decision, every action. Letting go felt risky. Uncomfortable.

Even irresponsible.

But letting go is a skill, and one many leaders either never learn or learn too late.

As Kenneth Blanchard puts it; "letting go is about empowering people by releasing control, trusting their abilities, and shifting focus from what's wrong to what's right". When that shift happens, micromanagement fades, and growth becomes possible.

I learned quickly that people don't like being micromanaged. Neither did I.

As trust grew and responsibility was shared, leadership stopped feeling like something I *put on* each day. It became a habit rather than a role.

I remember a conversation with one of the team, Kerry. I was talking about an article I'd been reading on modern management and leadership, and she looked at me and said, "You're a manager and a leader. You do this every day, and now you're learning about it as well?" She wasn't criticising. She was observing.

That comment stayed with me.

It highlighted a shift I hadn't fully recognised yet. Leadership was no longer something I was consciously trying to perform. It had become part of how I operated. How I showed up in conversations. How I made decisions. How I carried responsibility.

That realisation brought a quiet confidence. Not arrogance.

Not certainty. Just steadiness.

I still knew I didn't know everything. And I still don't.

A former CEO of mine at TAE Aerospace once said to me,
"Leadership and management are a bit like a computer game.
Some levels are easy. Some are challenging. And sometimes
you get it wrong. Just make sure you learn from the mistakes."
Thanks, Andrew.

That mindset changed how I led others, but also how I led
myself. Mistakes became feedback, not failure. Growth became
ongoing, not episodic. Leadership became less about control
and more about responsibility.

And that, for me, was the point where leadership stopped
feeling loud.

The Cost of Unconscious Leadership

One challenge that business owners, managers, leaders, and I
inevitably face is complacency.

After the successes at Airflite, it felt like the right time to
move on and further my career. I joined BAE Systems Australia,
working with 79 Squadron in support of the Hawk 127 Lead-
in Fighter trainer aircraft. Seven years at Airflite had been
formative. The challenges, the learning, the growth, both
professional and personal, had given me confidence. I knew
how to learn. I reflected regularly. I had systems. I was
evolving.

I was ready to take on the world.

What I discovered, very quickly, was that what worked for
one team would not necessarily work for another. Different
people. Different cultures. Different expectations. Different
definitions of success. While the supply chain is a supply chain

in a technical sense, leadership and business are never one-size-fits-all in practice.

My quiet confidence had become a blind spot.

I had assumed that competence would transfer cleanly. Those systems would behave the same way. That experience alone would carry me forward. In reality, I had stepped back to the beginning of the learning curve.

Again.

The only thing that saved me from failing outright was reflection.

I returned deliberately to the habits I had built. Daily review. Honest self-assessment. Adjusting my approach to the team and to the customer. Without that discipline, the transition would have been a disaster. It was still a rough road, uncomfortable, humbling, and at times frustrating, but progress came through reflection, the Plan–Do–Check–Act cycle, and the guidance of a trusted mentor.

Thanks, Bob.

Then in 2004, another change arrived. My wife informed me that we were moving to Queensland.

Once again, adaptation was required.

I successfully transferred to BAE Systems at Archerfield airport, supporting supply and deeper maintenance activities for the Iroquois helicopter, the Huey, a Vietnam-era aircraft operated by the Australian Army. Different platform. Different stakeholders. Different pressures. And once again, success depended not on what I already knew, but on my willingness to reflect, learn, and adapt.

In 2006, when Defence confirmed the retirement of the Huey fleet, I secured a role with Tasman Aviation Enterprises, at RAAF Amberley.

Change again. Reflect again. Adapt again. Succeed again.

The lesson was clear: unconscious leadership does not eliminate the need for conscious reflection. In fact, the more experienced you become, the greater the risk of assuming that yesterday's success will automatically translate into tomorrow's environment.

Success, left unchecked, can become complacency.

Unfortunately, complacency is often invisible to the person experiencing it.

Succeeding Is a Practice, Not a Peak

As discussed throughout this chapter, success is not a destination. It is a practice. When leaders focus solely on the destination, they may reach the goal and then stall. Growth stops. Learning slows. Reflection fades. Leadership becomes static. Businesses plateau. Unconscious leadership is not something you arrive at and keep forever; it only endures when it is continually exercised.

As Peter Drucker warned, *"The greatest danger in times of turbulence is not the turbulence; it is acting with yesterday's logic."* I learned that lesson firsthand. Turbulence is not an exception in business; it is the norm. Much like flying, some turbulence is barely noticeable, some test your confidence, and some make you grateful simply to land safely. The skill is not avoiding turbulence but learning how to operate within it.

Without reflection, without deliberately returning to Plan–Do–Check–Act, continued learning, and regular practice, leaders stop shaping outcomes and begin merely reacting to them. The goal should never disappear, but it must remain incremental. Each success should prompt the next question: *what's next?* In doing so, progress continues, learning compounds, and turbulence is contained to the phase in which it occurs. Sometimes the lesson is to adjust course. Sometimes it is to pause and re-route entirely. Either way, success remains a journey, one that demands attention, responsibility, and stewardship.

15

When success changes shape

When Success Changes Shape

By the time leaders reach unconscious competence, something subtle, nonetheless important, begins to happen. Problems don't disappear, but they change shape. The challenges are no longer about capability or effort. They're about continuity, resilience, and scale. What once required effort now requires design.

Success, more often than not, is not achieved alone. Some help arrives quietly in the background. Other support is offered openly. And yet many leaders are so focused on achieving the next goal that they don't see the bend in the road, the warning signs, or the people trying to help steady the journey.

Learning when to accept help — and when to ask for it — is one of the most difficult transitions leaders make.

I learned that lesson early.

I was five years old. Small for my age. Slight in stature. My mum and I were catching the bus. I dressed myself, put my socks on the right way, and even managed to get my shoes on the correct feet. I was proud, silly walk and all.

This was a big day.

For the first time ever, I was going to pay my own bus fare.

The bus pulled up. The doors opened. The driver smiled and waved. I reached into the pocket of my purple corduroy jeans, pulled out my fifty cents, and offered it to him.

Proud as punch.

He looked at me kindly and said, "It's okay, little mate. You don't have to pay until you're five."

I was offended.

How dare he suggest I wasn't five!

I stamped my foot and announced as loudly as I could, "I AM FIVE."

The passengers nearby giggled. The driver apologised with a grin. I probably embarrassed my mum.

What I didn't understand at the time was simple: the driver wasn't questioning my readiness. He was trying to help.

I was so focused on achieving my goal that I couldn't see help being offered.

We set goals, take action, and hit milestones. Support is offered, but often missed. Eventually, effort alone stops being enough.

The Little Critter books by Mercer Mayer capture this beautifully. In *When I Get Bigger*, Little Critter dreams of all the grown-up things he'll do one day. The story ends with a simple truth:

"But my mother says that I'm not bigger yet."

Leadership growth works the same way.

Around the same time, another memory surfaced.

Princess Margaret Hospital for Children is where I had surgery, physiotherapy, and ongoing check-ups. Each year, Channel 9 hosts Telethon to raise funds for children like me. During one of those broadcasts, John Farnham performed *Help*.

Here was a world-renowned Australian singer, standing on national television, singing a song called *Help*, to raise money for children he would never meet.

That moment stayed with me.

It reframed what help really meant.

Which brings me to business.

I once had a client state confidently during a risk discussion, "We don't have any risks. We're all covered."

I leaned back and said, "I can see a risk. You're just not aware that you've already described it. The risk is you."

The business owner experienced health issues and was out of action for six to eight weeks. During that time, the business lost six months' worth of revenue. There was no continuity plan. No system to carry on. No one could keep things moving while the owner recovered.

Unconscious leadership had taken them far. It just hadn't translated into resilience yet.

That's the moment when success actually changes shape.

What Unconscious Leadership Looks Like in Practice

In a growing SME, unconscious leadership becomes visible not through effort, but through absence. Decisions begin happening without the owner in the room. Problems are resolved before they escalate. Customers experience consistency rather than heroics.

And the leader is no longer the bottleneck.

I saw this clearly during my time at TAE Aerospace. In Manufacturing, we encountered an issue producing a sidewall plate for a chassis assembly. No matter what we did, it would not come out square. In aerospace, being out by one-thousandth of an inch is unacceptable.

The team walked methodically through every step. Everything appeared correct.

I didn't diagnose. I didn't intervene. I simply asked questions and left space.

The following day, the team discovered the CNC bed was out by one-thousandth of an inch. Once adjusted, the issue disappeared.

What mattered wasn't the question I asked. It was what I didn't do.

That's unconscious leadership in practice. The work gets done, the problem is solved, and the leader is no longer the constraint.

When Help Becomes Strategic

For a long time, I believed helping meant taking more on myself. In reality, I was becoming the bottleneck — not through lack of capability, but through reluctance to let go.

A respected colleague once said to me, simply, "You're stressed."

The next day, when he asked again, I finally admitted it.

That was the moment I realised my leadership had become the bottleneck. Not because I lacked capability, but because I hadn't yet learned to let go.

When I stepped back from doing and focused on observing, listening, and enabling, something shifted. Firefighting reduced. Decisions steadied. Momentum returned.

As we learned in school science, the greater the friction, the less the momentum.

Success didn't come from more effort.

It came from removing what was slowing us down.

This is where help changes form.

Early in leadership, help feels emotional; It arrives in moments of fatigue or overwhelm. Later, help becomes strategic. Mentors are sounding boards. Advisors prevent problems rather than fix them. Ecosystems become structural, not optional.

Success isn't about needing less help.

It's about using it better.

The Continuity Lens

At a certain point in an SMEs journey, success raises different questions.

Not *"How do we grow?"*

But *"What survives us?"*

This is where leadership begins to shift from competence into something else.

From doing to designing.

From control to continuity.

From achievement to stewardship.

This doesn't mean stepping away.

It means stepping differently.

That is where the next phase of leadership begins.

16

Success to stewardship

From Success to Stewardship

Success, as we've discussed throughout this book, is the achievement of a goal or a desired outcome. But stewardship asks a different question altogether: *what survives you once that outcome has been achieved?*

For me, stewardship stopped being theoretical when I realised that success wasn't about what I could personally deliver, but what continued to function once I stepped back.

At Airflite, that meant building a team that was united, capable, and trusted to make decisions, and just as importantly, trusted to learn from their mistakes. The team knew I was there to guide and support them, but they also knew they didn't need permission for every step. Ownership had begun to shift.

One moment stands out clearly.

One of my team members, the wife of a technician also working at Airflite, was one of the strongest contributors in the group and a close colleague. In a small town like Bullsbrook, the boundary between work and life isn't always neat. One morning, I noticed something was off as she walked past my office. I simply called out, "Do you have a minute?"

She came in. I closed the door, looked her in the eye, and asked, "Are you OK?"

She paused, then said, "You're the only person who can tell when I'm not."

That moment stayed with me. Not because of what I said, but because of what continued after I left. And it reminded me that leadership leaves marks we don't always see at the time.

When I later moved to 79 Squadron, this same person stepped into a supervisory role. What gave me genuine pride wasn't the title she held; it was watching the culture continue. The care for the team. The trust. The willingness to nurture capability rather than control behaviour. What we had built together survived my departure.

That, to me, was stewardship in action.

There is an old saying that leadership failures show themselves from the top down. It's uncomfortable, but largely true. Leaders and business owners shape not only outcomes, but environments, through what they tolerate, what they model, and what they choose to step back from. That responsibility doesn't disappear when success arrives. If anything, it becomes heavier.

I learned that if I wasn't investing in people, systems, and decision-making that could outlast my presence, then I wasn't really leading; I was simply passing through.

True leadership isn't proven by how indispensable you are. It's proven by how well things function when you're not there.

That's when success matures into stewardship, and when legacy stops being something you talk about and becomes something others carry forward.

Sometimes, Things Don't Go to Plan

Stewardship is not proven when things go to plan.

It's revealed when the plan disappears. I was racing BMX in Karratha.

Up on the starting mound, ten of us lined up. The siren sounded, the gate dropped, and we were off. We hit the first corner together, a tight pack of riders fighting for position.

Then it happened.

Someone clipped another rider's rear wheel, and in an instant, nine of us were on the ground.

Bikes tangled. Dust everywhere. Bodies piled up.

One rider stayed upright and kept going.

I untangled myself, jumped back on my bike, put my head down, and pedalled with everything I had. I didn't think about the crash. I didn't think about how far behind I was. I just rode.

As I pushed harder, I noticed something unexpected.

The leader was sitting down, coasting towards the finish line.

Comfortable. Confident. Certain the race was already won.

I saw my chance.

The crowd started screaming. I could hear them yelling at the leader, warning them I was closing fast. I was gaining ground, bike length by bike length. I could see the finish line. I could almost taste it.

Three bike lengths away, the leader looked back, stood up, and pedalled away.

The race announcer's voice cut through the noise:

"And here comes Kenny Newton, number 400!"

I crossed the line in second place.

It was the highest finish I ever achieved in BMX racing.

Did I succeed in winning the race? No.

Did I stay in the race after the crash? Yes.

The applause wasn't for first place.

It was for resilience.

Long after the podium is forgotten, what endures is how you respond when the plan disappears.

Systems as Memory

If stewardship asks what survives you, systems answer a quieter question: what does the business remember when you're not there?

Remember the business owner from our risk discussion—the one who learned they were the risk themselves? Without systems, their absence revealed the gap: no continuity plan meant the business stalled, losing six months' revenue in weeks.

That gap became the catalyst. We reframed systems not as paperwork or red tape, but as *stored decision-making*—processes embedding day-to-day choices in habits, checklists, and roles anyone could follow.

The transformation was swift. Today, that same business handles both ongoing work and new inbound leads seamlessly, even without the owner present. The leader just took an overseas holiday, genuinely switching off for the first time. Decisions now live in people, processes, and shared memory, not one exhausted mind.

That is what good systems do. They protect teams from individual stress, mood, and availability. They allow consistency without constant supervision. They turn leadership intent into something others can carry.

Ecosystems extend this idea further.

Just as natural ecosystems rely on interdependence, business ecosystems provide continuity beyond the organisation itself. Accountants, lawyers, advisors, coaches, and specialists are not optional extras. At a certain stage, they become part of the system's memory, available when the business needs support that shouldn't live internally.

I saw this clearly when a client felt pressured to sign an expensive third-party HR agreement driven by legislative requirements and a lack of timely advice. At the moment, the decision felt urgent. But urgency is not the same as necessity.

Because the business had a functioning ecosystem, we were able to pause. Review the terms. Understand the risk properly. Disengage legally. And then secure exactly the support required, nothing more, nothing less. The outcome wasn't just financial savings. It was confidence. The system worked even under pressure.

Systems are not bureaucracy. They are how stewardship becomes repeatable. They hold judgement when people are tired. They protect teams from panic. They ensure that when a leader steps away, the business doesn't forget how to move forward. That's stewardship made tangible.

The Shift from Doing to Holding

If leadership is professional growth, and learning from mistakes is personal growth, then the shift from *doing* to *holding* is one of the steepest learning curves of all. It challenges both instinct and identity.

Most leaders are wired to act. To step in. To help. To fix. For years, that instinct has been rewarded. But at a certain point, the very behaviour that once created momentum begins to limit it.

Stewardship requires a different posture.

Leaving a legacy means resisting the urge to correct every misstep and instead creating the conditions where others can make good decisions themselves and learn when they don't. The responsibility shifts from *preventing mistakes* to *reinforcing what works.* It's about catching people doing the right thing and strengthening that behaviour.

This approach is a long way from the leadership model I was trained under. During recruit training in the late 1980's, the message was clear: "You'll only hear from me when you do something wrong." That model produced compliance. It didn't produce ownership.

My real shift began at Airflite and deepened during my time at TAE Aerospace. The urge to intervene was constant, especially during complex work like the ERP replacement project. But every time I stepped back and allowed the team to work through decisions themselves, something changed. Confidence grew.

Judgement sharpened. Ownership took hold.

The closest analogy I can offer is teaching your child to drive. You're no longer in control; they are. You can offer guidance, reassurance, and boundaries, but you can't take the wheel without undoing the lesson. All the while, you're pressing an imaginary brake pedal and white-knuckling the door handle. That restraint is the work.

They start holding: standards, intent, safety. They create space. In that space, people rise. You can see it physically.

Posture changes. Pride appears. Decisions become more considered.

Strength at this stage doesn't come from action.

It comes from choosing, deliberately, when not to intervene.

Legacy Without Ego

There is a quote often attributed to Peter Strople that has stayed with me:

"Legacy is not leaving something behind for other people. It's leaving something behind in other people."

That idea resonates deeply with me, particularly at this stage of leadership. Because real legacy rarely looks like recognition. It doesn't arrive with applause, awards, or farewell speeches. More often, it shows up quietly, long after you've stepped back.

When leadership matures, systems begin to hold what the leader once carried. Procedures, habits, language, and expectations become second nature. Decisions are made without escalation. Problems are addressed without drama. People know what "good" looks like, not because it's written on a wall, but because they've lived it. At that point, the leader's role is no longer to be visible; it's to be felt.

Success without ego is learning to step back and watch others apply principles you once had to teach explicitly. It's seeing teams solve problems in ways you would have solved them, or sometimes better. It's recognising that your influence is present even when your name is not.

True success isn't measured by how much credit you receive. It's measured by what continues when you're not there to intervene. When no one is applauding. When nothing needs fixing. When the business simply works.

If I reflect on what I would want people to say about working in my business, it isn't about performance metrics or outcomes alone. I hope they would say that it felt safe. That they were trusted. That they were supported to grow. That they were allowed to make mistakes and learn from them. That they were treated as people first, not resources.

Because legacy isn't announced.

It's experienced.

And when leadership reaches that point, success is no longer something you chase; it's something you leave behind.

A Pause Before You Turn the Page

If you paused here for a moment, it wouldn't be to analyse what you've read, it would be to notice what's already familiar.

You may recognise parts of your own journey in these pages. The improvisation. The adaptation. The quiet successes that didn't look dramatic at the time but mattered more than you realised. You may even notice that some of what you thought you were still striving for is already taking shape.

Perhaps the questions that matter most now aren't about what to do next, but about what's already being built.

What will remain when you step back?

Where are decisions already happening without you?

How does it feel for people to work with you, not just for you?

Are you still rushing to help, or learning when to hold?

And when support is offered, are you open enough to receive it?

You don't need to answer these questions today. Awareness

is enough.

If this book has offered anything of value, I hope it's this: a sense that success isn't always loud, visible, or complete. Often, it's quiet. It's embedded. Sometimes it's already closer than we think.

As the Beatles once sang, *"my independence has vanished in the haze"*, not as a loss, but as a recognition that none of us succeed alone.

When you're ready, you can turn the page.

The journey doesn't end here; it simply continues with clearer eyes.

Closing the Loop: Improvise → Adapt → Succeed

Dear reader, what you've just reflected on is personal — what follows is the lens I've used to make sense of it.

There comes a point on any long journey where it's worth stopping, not to rest, but to look back. Not to admire the path, but to recognise how far you've actually come. Sometimes you don't realise the ground you've covered until you pause and see the trail behind you.

Improvising was once imagination and escape, finding ways to create something from nothing. Today, it's how I help clients find options when the obvious ones have run out.

Adapting was once about surviving change, moving from the city to Nanutarra Station, learning new environments, new rules, new rhythms. Now, it's about helping businesses adjust deliberately to the environments they operate in, rather than being shaped by them.

Success wasn't something I consciously chased growing up. School was school. Results were "good enough." Even later, success was often defined by outcomes alone: a race finished, a role secured, a goal achieved. Today, success looks different. It's watching others grow. It's seeing teams step forward with confidence. It's witnessing the legacy others are building long after you've stepped back.

Improvise → Adapt → Succeed means something very different to me now than it did when I was five, seven, ten, or seventeen. I was living it long before I could name it, and it became my framework well before it ever became my motto.

Through learning to walk again, remote living and rigid systems. Through uniforms, routines, and eventually leadership. It was there even when I wasn't aware of it.

If there's one hope I leave you with, it's this: that somewhere in these pages, you recognised yourself - and where you are now.

The Tools in Part IV make it real. Pick one. Run the Continuity Lens with your team. Or the 30-Day Test solo. Forward motion matters. Especially when things don't go as expected…

When the plaster wears thin, the donkey isn't lit, or the crash happens mid-race, you remember that forward motion still matters.

Sometimes success isn't winning, it's getting back up, putting your head down, and staying in the race.

17

End of Part Three – Putting Stewardship to Work

Stewardship is success that doesn't depend on you. It's when the business hums, decisions get made, problems get solved, culture holds, whether you're in the building or on holiday.

This final section asks you to view through a stewardship lens. Not to step away tomorrow, but to notice where your leadership has already created something that outlasts your presence.

Where Stewardship is Taking Shape

First, spot the good signs. Stewardship shows up when:

- Decisions happen at the right level without your input.
- The team can handle both current work and new opportunities when you're unavailable.
- The culture feels consistent, with care for people, trust in judgement, and ownership of outcomes.

- You've taken time away, and things didn't just survive; they progressed.

Note two recent examples where this felt true.

- What was the situation?
- Who stepped up?
- What made it work without you directing?

These aren't accidents. They're evidence that your leadership is maturing into something others can carry.

Where Stewardship Still Needs Attention

Now look for gaps. Stewardship lags when success still feels personal rather than embedded.

Key signals:

- Your absence results in a visible slowdown in productivity or a drop in quality.
- "The risk is you" still applies; no one else can pick up key decisions or relationships.
- Systems handle routine but buckle under new volume, complexity, or change.
- The team knows how to process today's work but not how to create tomorrow's pipeline.
- Boards or advisors ask, "What happens if [you] aren't there?"

Mark the top two. These are where small shifts in design, not increased effort, build resilience.

Questions For Leaders, Boards, and Trusted Advisors

Use these alone, in an executive huddle, or with a trusted advisor:

- If I stepped back for eight weeks, what would stop first: cash, pipeline, delivery, or decisions?
- Where do we still need me because no one else carries that judgement, or relationship?
- What three decisions happen without me that used to need my sign-off?
- Does our culture live in processes, habits, and people? Or just in my stories and examples?
- What survives us? Be specific: name the mechanisms, not the hope.

The answers reveal where stewardship lies and where it needs to be embedded.

One Experiment: Test Continuity

Choose one area where your presence is still the hinge. Test this over the next six weeks:

- Name the outcome (e.g., "new client quotes approved," "weekly cash position clear").
- Capture the 3–5 key steps or principles on one page. Write it like you would to a capable newcomer.
- Hand it to one or two others. Let them run it five times. Debrief: "What was missing? What was clear?"
- Tweak once based on their input. Repeat.

No fanfare. No full roll out. Just proof that decisions can live outside you.

If it holds, stewardship grows. If it reveals gaps, you know exactly where to focus.

That's stewardship in action.

Improvisation got you moving. Adaptation made it repeatable. Stewardship ensures it endures.

You've built something worth leaving behind. Now make sure it doesn't need you to keep going.

IV

Tools

*The stories and reflections in this book are from real life, both my own and the businesses I've worked with. But stories alone don't build capability. This section gives you the tools to turn **Improvise → Adapt → Succeed** into something your team can use. No theory. No complexity. Just simple ways to notice where you are, where you're heading, and what to do next. Take what works. Leave the rest.*

18

Continuity & Stewardship Lens

This tool provides a simple way to see where your business sits between **early improvisation**, **adaptation**, and **true stewardship**. It's not a test with right or wrong answers. It's a lens to help you notice what's working, what's settling, and where small changes create lasting capability.

Think of it as four levels of maturity across five key areas. Most businesses aren't at one level across the board; they're a mixture and that's normal. The value is in spotting patterns and selecting one or two places to strengthen.

The Four Levels

1. Improvising

Everything works through effort, relationships, or being there yourself. Progress happens, but it depends on you or a few key people.

Common in startups, family businesses, or rapid growth phases.

2. Adapting

Some things are repeatable. You've captured what works in routines or simple guides. Things feel steadier, but scale or change still reveals gaps.

Common when stabilising after growth or disruption.

3. Established

Most decisions have clear ownership and simple processes. The business continues to operate without continued intervention, but leadership remains heavily involved.

Common in mature SMEs ready for their next leap.

4. Stewardship

The business operates with or without you. Decisions, culture, and continuity live in systems, people, and habits. Leadership focuses on direction, not delivery.

Where success becomes legacy.

The Five Dimensions

Use the table below to mark where your business sits **today**. Be honest, not critical. Jot a quick note or example next to each.

Dimension	Improvising (Level 1)	Adapting (Level 2)	Established (Level 3)	Stewardship (Level 4)
Leadership	You make most decisions. Team waits for direction.	Some decisions delegate naturally. You approve key ones.	Right people make right calls without escalation.	Leadership sets direction. Execution lives elsewhere.
Systems	Workarounds for everything. Knowledge in heads.	Basic routines for core work. Gaps show under pressure.	Clear processes for 80% of work. Flexible for the rest.	Systems as memory—handle routine + create new work.
Ecosystem	Solo or small circle. Gaps filled internally.	Key advisors (accountant, lawyer). Used reactively.	Proactive network. Gaps spotted early.	Interdependence. External capability treated as core.
People	Heroics get results. Consistency varies by person.	Roles clear. Skills growing. Still personality driven.	Capability consistent. Culture shapes behaviour.	Ownership embedded. People develop each other.
Continuity	Your absence = slowdown or stall. No backup for you.	Team manages current work. New work slows.	Business progresses without you short-term.	Thrives long-term. Pipeline, cash, culture all intact.

How to use it:

1. Read each row. Mark your current level (1-4).
2. Note 1-2 examples that confirm it.
3. Look across columns. Where do patterns cluster?
4. Pick **one dimension** to strengthen by one level.

Reading Your Results

Mostly 1s (Improvising): You're moving, which matters. Next step: capture 2-3 key routines so others can run them. Start small, quoting, invoicing, and weekly cash reviews.

Mix of 1s and 2s (Transitioning): Adaptation is taking hold. Focus on the dimension with the most 1. Write one page: "If I'm away, here's how [X] keeps moving."

Mostly 2 and 3 (Established): Solid base. Stewardship lives in continuity and an ecosystem. Test: take four weeks off. What needs embedding?

3 and 4 (Stewardship): Rare and valuable. Ask: "What survives us?" Document it. Share it. Let it become your legacy.

Making It Real: Three Next Steps

No grand project. Pick one.
Step 1: Continuity Check (30 minutes)
If I were unavailable for eight weeks, rank these by risk:

- Cash flow
- New client pipeline
- Key deliveries
- Team decisions
- Pick the #1 risk. Write the 3-5 steps someone else needs to run it. Test next month.

Step 2: Stewardship Conversation (1 hour)
With your leadership team or trusted advisor, ask:

- "What three things would stall without [me]?"
- "Where do we improvise that should be adapted?"
- "What's one routine we could make repeatable this quarter?"
- Write the answers. Act on one.

Step 3: Ecosystem Gap Spot (solo)
List your top three external relationships (accountant, lawyer,

HR, advisor).

For each: When did we last use them proactively? What gap could they fill?

Schedule one conversation this month.

Why This Works

This lens isn't about perfection,it's about direction. Businesses don't jump levels—they climb them, one deliberate step at a time.

You've already done the hard work of improvising and adapting. This tool simply helps you see where stewardship awaits.

The stories in this book showed you it's possible.

These steps show you that it's practical.

One level at a time. That's how capability compounds.

19

Workshop and Guided Discussion

This Work Was Never Meant To Be Completed Alone.

Reflection creates awareness.

Conversation creates alignment.

At a certain point, the questions stop being about insight and start becoming about interpretation, judgement, and choice. That's where solo thinking reaches its natural limit.

In my experience, the most meaningful shifts don't come from filling in worksheets or following steps. They come from shared language, challenge, and the safety to test ideas out loud.

This is why the framework lives best in dialogue — where assumptions can be surfaced, perspectives can collide productively, and decisions can be held up to scrutiny before they're acted on.

If these chapters have surfaced complexity rather than clarity, that's not a sign you've missed something. It's usually a sign that the work is ready to move from reflection into conversation.

20

30-Day Continuity Test

From Insight to Continuity

A thirty-day test isn't about discipline.

It's about exposure.

Over time, patterns reveal themselves, such as:

- What holds without you?
- What slows when attention is diverted?
- What collapses when pressure is applied?

Most leaders don't fail this kind of examination; they simply notice more than they expected.

Because continuity isn't revealed in intention, it's revealed in repetition.

For some, recognising these patterns is enough.

For others, the moment of recognition raises questions that

are not resolved easily in isolation.

Not because capability is missing, but because perspective sharpens when it's shared.

If reading this has made certain dependencies, risks, or assumptions more visible, particularly those tied to your own presence, that awareness isn't a problem to solve.

It's usually a signal that the work is ready to move from reflection into deliberate examination.

About the author

Ken Newton is a leadership practitioner, business advisor, and systems thinker with more than two decades of experience operating in complex, high-consequence environments.

His career spans Defence aviation acquisition and sustainment, enterprise systems implementation, end-to-end supply chain leadership, and executive advisory work across asset-intensive and highly regulated organisations. He has led teams through disruption, ERP transformation, operational restructuring, and periods where continuity, judgement, and people mattered more than speed or certainty.

Ken is known for his ability to work alongside leaders in a way that is practical, adaptive, and deeply human. Rather than imposing models or rigid frameworks, he takes time to understand how individuals and organisations actually operate, then selectively applies structure, experience, and disciplined thinking to help them move forward with clarity and intent.

Clients consistently describe him as patient, considered, and solution-oriented — someone who brings both commercial realism and personal steadiness to complex decisions. His work focuses on strengthening leadership capability, embedding systems that endure, and helping organisations transition from individual success into collective stewardship.

Ken holds an MBA, is a Certified Professional Business Advisor, and a Registered Practitioner of Integrated Product

Support. He works with business owners, executives, and institutions navigating complexity, structural change, and long-term capability development.

He regularly facilitates executive workshops and leadership discussions grounded in the *Improvise → Adapt → Succeed* framework.

Improvise → Adapt → Succeed is his first book.

www.ingramcontent.com/pod-product-compliance
Lightning Source LLC
Chambersburg PA
CBHW071639030726
47592CB00008B/2861